WITHDRAWN

A PRIMER FOR CHOREOGRAPHERS

Lois Ellfeldt

University of Southern California

Illustrations by Sue Powell

MAYFIELD PUBLISHING COMPANY

Library of Congress Catalog Card Number: 67-20074
International Standard Book Numbers: 0-87484-192-5 *(paper)*
0-87484-124-0 *(cloth)*
Manufactured in the United States of America

Mayfield Publishing Company
285 Hamilton Avenue
Palo Alto, California 94301

FOREWORD

Choreographers do not make dances out of words. They compose them in the vocabulary of movement. Dr. Ellfeldt has long demonstrated her command of that vocabulary in her own dance compositions. Now, in *A Primer for Choreographers,* she has undertaken the difficult task of explaining its alphabet to beginning students.

Well aware that this alphabet is meaningful only in its own movement terms, she has used words sparingly. Rather than verbalizing about the properties of movement as a medium for communication, she has made it possible for students to discover the ABC's of dance in a series of movement experiences. In this way, she has provided functional answers to the persistent questions of all would-be choreographers: How do I start? How do I find a movement-provoking idea? How do I find a movement? How do I put the idea and the movement together to make a dance? And so on through all of the troublesome questions about spatial relationships, visual images, settings, accompaniment, and other considerations that enter into a meaningful dance composition.

The sense of these discoveries is well illustrated in the series of drawings prepared by Sue Powell, for the illustrator is also a choreographer who has worked with many beginning students in the dance studio.

By calling this book a *Primer,* the writer and the illustrator have identified it as an elementary textbook for students who are just beginning to compose their own dances. But this exposition of the basic principles of choreography is much more than an elementary text. It is also a substantial contribution to the choreographic literature and to the growing body of literature dealing with the meaningful properties of movement in all its forms. As such, it may well be read with profit by experienced choreographers and dancers, and by anyone interested in movement as a source of meaning in human life.

Eleanor Metheny
Los Angeles, California
May, 1967

PREFACE

A choreographer is a maker of dances, and his creations exist, finally, as sequences of movement on a stage. Yet in any medium, a work of art is something more than elements of sound, design, or movement arranged in a pattern or sequence. Behind the process of craftsmanship is the personality of the creator – the living, reacting, concerned human being who makes images with the materials at his command.

Even a child can say, "I just made up a dance." Possibly he has. "Dance" is not a scientific term, with a tidy meaning. The definition of "dance" is often most unclear to those who most yearn to contribute to the art. In high schools, colleges, studios, camps, community centers, and family rooms, potential choreographers wonder: "What do you do *first* when you make up a dance?"

This book begins with a brief definition of dance, and supplies the young dancer, not with an easy explanation of the process of choreography, but with some tools for finding his own process. It is a primer, a beginner's book, which identifies, as it were, the alphabet and the rules of grammar and spelling of dance. It is not a how-to-do-it book, for no one is sure how to succeed as a choreographer – except, in the colloquial phrase, by really trying!

The neophyte may learn a great deal from seeing, analyzing, and performing the choreography of mature artists, and from studying with good teachers, but he must nonetheless find *his own way* if he is to do anything creative. Broadened horizons of discrimination and control of movement are necessary only when they are meaningful to the choreographer and functional to the particular problem at hand – not as an end in themselves.

I have simply set down some guidelines for the beginner, as he starts his venture into the highly personal and thoroughly creative business of "making up dances."

Lois Ellfeldt
Laguna Beach, California
July, 1967

ACKNOWLEDGMENTS

After three decades in dance, my list of acknowledgments is long and necessarily incomplete: I remember with particular gratitude Marian Chace and Lester Shafer, then of the Denishawn school; Ruth Aubeck at George Washington University; Charlotte MacEwan at Wellesley College; the Bennington years with Martha Hill, Louis Horst, John Martin, Martha Graham, Doris Humphrey, Charles Weidman, Hanya Holm, and Ruth and Norman Lloyd; and the German venture with Mary Wigman and Rudolf von Laban. I owe special appreciation and affection to Doris Humphrey and Charles Weidman for the exciting experience of dancing with their group and of knowing them as people as well as artist-teachers. To the members of my own dance group, and to all those students who shared with me happy and fruitful years of choreography and performance—my gratitude and personal regard.

Nor can I forget Eleanor Metheny for the long hours of discussion spent untangling ideas about dance as a human activity; Claude Chidamian for his insistent regard for simplicity and direct communication; Sue Powell for her sensitive and imaginative illustrations; Judy Bare, National Press editor, for her insight, concern, and ability to make sense of the manuscript; and Leah Ellfeldt, my mother, for her encouragement, assistance, and patient understanding through it all.

CONTENTS

"The teaching of art is the only subject in his educational experience where a member of the future generation can be offered the chance to truly find himself as a unique person; because only here are there no ready-made answers telling him what he ought to see, feel, think or in which way he ought to find his self-realization."—BRUNO BETTELHEIM*

*"Art: A Personal Vision," in *Art* (New York: The Museum of Modern Art, 1962 [produced for the National Committee on Art Education, and distributed by Doubleday and Co., New York]), p. 62.

1
From the Beginning . . .
DANCE

The very word "dance" denotes motion. But the dictionary supplies an assortment of subsidiary definitions: "to perform a rhythmic and patterned succession of movements"; "to move nimbly and merrily"; and sometimes "to cause to dance." Since a choreographer causes others to dance, it is well to begin this primer with a working definition of the word. For dance, clearly, is many things! Some people "dance for joy" when the stock market rises. On a summer evening the fireflies "dance through the trees." A desert whirlwind "dances across the dusty mesa." The birds "dance," we are told, as do moonbeams, flowers, soap powders, grunions, and atoms. An infant, after a healthy yell, sets out on his "dance of life"—and our thoughts "dance" to consider it all.

However, dance has come to be associated primarily with unusual patterns of movement. Although the word retains a variety of meanings, it is commonly used to label any action that is lively or exotic. In most cases it describes a kind of planned and rhythmic motion, but practically everything that living creatures do is patterned and rhythmic! Just what kind of movement is *dance movement*? When does it cease being the movement of play, work, or random act and become the movement of dance? The movement itself does not change, of course. It is only selected and patterned to serve certain characteristic purposes. Sometimes the difference between dance and another activity is obvious; sometimes it seems slight or even nonexistent.

In all human action, what is done must occur in accordance with the mechanical principles of movement. With wide variation in efficiency, man moves his body by directing neuromuscular energy to overcome gravity and the inertia of his body weight. Therefore, the movement of dance is much like the movement of any other human activity; the principles and problems are the same. Also like other movement experiences, dance exists simultaneously in both time and space. Regardless of purpose, then, the definition of "what effort . . . to go where . . . when" gives the movement sequence its form. Indeed, the factors of time, space, and energy operate whether they are used consciously or unconsciously.

But man is more than nerves and muscles in space and time: he moves to fulfill a purpose. It is that purpose which distinguishes one sort of dance from another, whether in one period or through history. The purposes of dance have changed as human culture has changed, for dance is created by individuals who belong to a particular milieu. The art probably began as embellished action, selected and organized not for private reasons, but as a rite of evocative magic. Primitive man danced to appease his gods. Eventually, dance served tribal rituals, rather than sacred rites. As civilization evolved, dance became part of folk culture; it expressed ethnic distinctions and nationalistic convictions. In more modern times, dance has assumed many forms, with many aims.

First of all, it can be social or recreational. The boy-and-girl fun of dance probably originated in the primitive fertility rite (the "coming of age dance") or in other tribal ceremonies that have their contemporary counterparts in the debutante's ball, the senior prom, the latest dance craze, or the polka party at the ski lodge. **SOCIAL DANCE**

Dance today also can be nationalistic or ethnic. Remnants of nationalistic styles of movement are usually called folk dance. Although it has lost much of its original nationalistic intent, folk dance continues in festival displays or in arbitrary examples of the "authentic dances" of a particular folk. While social dance is also a folk form, in the sense that it is done by ordinary people, it is enjoyed as a contemporary experience. A distinguishing character- **FOLK DANCE** istic of "folk dance" is its traditional form as an expression of nationalism. On the other hand, ethnic dance presents the distinctly cultural, sometimes racial, and often religious character of a peo-

ETHNIC DANCE

ple. Most of the "ethnic dance" today has been diluted and rearranged for theater audiences, and so it has acquired an entirely different intent. For example, at the summer display at the Indian Roundup in Gallup, New Mexico, the Osage-Pawnee Dance of Greeting, Zuñi Hoop Dance, Hopi Antelope Dance, Plains War Dance, and Navajo Squaw Dance follow one another like old-time vaudeville acts. The genuine ethnic dance takes its place and time of performance from the framework of the culture of which it is a part; it is not performed as a tourist attraction.

SPECTACULAR DANCE

The major image of dance, however, at least in the popular mind, is that of spectacular dance. Its purpose is primarily to bedazzle the audience by augmenting a literal or musical theme, by arousing erotic feelings, or by displaying a performer's technical virtuosity. As a part of the make-believe of theater, such dance entertains, but it is a thing of the moment. It adds nothing to the viewer's store of emotional or aesthetic experience.

There are many kinds of spectacular dancers—the magnificently disciplined *corps de ballet*, the couple with straw hats and canes doing a soft-shoe routine, the precise Rockettes, the charming children's chorus in *The King and I*, and the barefoot modern dancer performing unusual feats of movement magic. And there are many things displayed—the nimble feet of the tap dancers, the exquisite skill of the *première danseuse* in the ballet, the flexible necks of Hindu-jazz dancers, the legs and panties of cancan girls, the befeathered and bespangled skin of chorus girls, and the tricks of a devotee of brilliant technique. But dance as an art form serves a different purpose. The artistic act is a conscious expression of an artist's comment on his world.

Such dance is a language, a special kind of a language. There are no words, nor is there a literal message in the language of dance. It is not an avenue of factual information, nor is it simply entertainment. Of course, it can be these things, but only incidentally. The words that dance "speaks" are movement phrases expressive of a choreographer's design. Dance is a statement, an expression in movement, containing some comment on reality that endures after the dance is over. One might say that dance as an art creates movement images through which we may become more sensitive to reality. It is an experience to provide enrichment and growth—for both the artist and his audience.

The dancer's instrument of communication is his own body. The proficiency required of him, the technical skill demanded in manipulating that body, may vary according to the style of a particular type of dance. However, contemporary dance sets no arbitrary limits upon degree of skill or type of action. The only restriction to movement potential is that imposed by anatomical or physiological factors, and *any* movement is a possible source of dance material.

In addition to proficiency in moving his body about a fixed base, carrying it through space with turns, leaps into the air, or falls to the floor, and bringing it into complex relationships with other people and with space, a dancer must be able to control his effort so that he can move to where he wants to be – at the time he wants to be there. Therefore, the first question a dancer asks is: how can I direct and control effort and channel my energy?

THE USE OF ENERGY

The term *energy*, as applied to dance, describes an exertion which initiates, controls, and stops movement. Such factors as *intensity, accent,* and *quality* of movement can be recognized only in relative terms. What, for example, is strong? What is smooth and unaccented? Only when the dynamics of movement are contrasted can we see any particular character of movement.

Energy-change arouses "feelings" within both the dancer and the audience. The exact meanings associated with the change are impossible to identify. Nonetheless, dramatic implications are always present. Aspects of the action and the people concerned in it may alter these implications. An audience, for example, is affected differently by a controlled, integrated effort than by a random and uncoordinated splash of energy.

ENERGY: INTENSITY   When a dancer moves, he can exert more or less intensity, with gradations ranging from almost imperceptible tension to a violent burst of energy. A tremendous display of force provides an action full of vigor and drive. However, although a strong movement implies greater size, it need not take any more space than a weak one. Conversely, less energy subordinates excitement and affirmation, and often results in a "contained" expression.

Accent occurs when some stress of either greater or lesser force is displayed. Often it is a contrast to what has been happening, or it is an "attention-getting" device. Accent is a tool for differentiating and identifying the pattern and rhythm of a particular motion. A regular accent creates a balanced and secure feeling. Irregular accents of varying intensity create a disturbing, confusing effect.

ENERGY: ACCENT

The quality of a dance movement is determined by the way energy is used. For instance, a *swinging movement* falls with gravity, gains momentum, and moves in an opposing arc until gravity once again causes a fall. The length of the body part that is falling and the nature of the joint and the supporting tissue all combine to determine the speed and rhythm of the action. That is, the swing of an arm or leg is more facile than the swing of an entire torso. There is a repetitive character to such a swing, which may recur as regularly as the motion of the pendulum in a Grandfather's clock.

ENERGY: QUALITY

Another quality is provided by *percussive movement*, which has very obvious starts and stops, with no continuity. It repeats jabs of energy with marked accents. It easily provokes emotional overtones of excitement and nervousness.

Sustained movement appears to flow, with no obvious beginning or ending. It has only unaccented continuity, with nothing to break the smooth progression of directed energy.

Vibratory movement is really a continuum of percussive movements, a repetition of individual start-and-stop patterns. There is an hypnotic effect in such movement, as in a persistent jitter.

Suspension occurs at that point of resistance to gravity where, for an instant—as at the height of a leap or just before a fall—the dancer seems to be suspended in space. The emotional excitement is generated by the sense of unreality inherent in such defiance of gravity. Probably no more dramatic or potentially powerful quality is to be found in movement.

Seldom is any one of these movement qualities found in a pure form in dance. Usually, there is a combination of several identifiable qualities, each with its own dramatic overtones.

IN SPACE

Movement exists in space, which, to a dancer, means a potential of position and dimension. Position includes the dancer's level in regard to the floor surface and the direction in which he is moving. Dimension refers to the size of the dancer's movement. *Direction, level,* and *size* are clearly relative terms. Where, for example, is forward? How high is up? Only when some standard is established can we recognize differences.

To illustrate, size is related to the dancer's range of movement both in space and on the floor surface. An increase in size, which often has dramatic implications of breadth and scope, is relative to the movement that has gone before, and it is limited by the total stage space available.

Direction, level, and size relate to the perspective of the audience as well as to the space of the stage. If the performer is on a traditional stage, there is a characteristic set of spatial problems which are predetermined by the stage. Any given performing area contains its own assets and liabilities of perspective and dimension. It is obvious that a choreographer must be keenly aware of the prospective performance area as he designs a dance movement. If the stage is not available, then its size and shape should be marked off in the studio.

SPACE: AUDIENCE PERSPECTIVE

A choreographer should explore the power and weakness of moving and stationary figures on every part of the stage area. Exits and entrances should be examined from all possible places, the dancers' focus of force should be determined, and varying numbers of dancers should be observed in different relationships, both to each other and to the peculiarities of stage perspective. It is not enough to design a dance movement; it is imperative that it be designed for the area where it will be performed. Of course, the magic is created by *what* is done in space. Nonetheless, any movement, however potentially powerful it may be, cannot create its full impact when it is done in an unsuitable space.

It is important to remember that moving figures create designs in space, and—beyond this visual effect—relationships between movement and space evoke shades of meaning. When the dancer appears to control space, clearly the meaning evoked by his action itself is augmented by that fact that his action affects the space. Both the visual and connotational effects must be recognized.

SPACE:
LEVEL
For instance, as a dancer *elevates* his body he is limited only by his own power and leverage. He reaches his greatest height in

a jump or leap, and his lowest level in a fall onto the floor. Dramatic implications abound in the exhilaration of soaring into the heights, contrasted with the sure fall to earth.

The four corners of the rectangular box stage form a frame of reference for the position and action of the dancers. To the audience, upstage appears remote and deep in the distance; downstage, as it fans out broadly, is closer, and therefore more intimate.

If interconnecting lines were drawn from the vertical corners of the stage box, one could see the diagonal lines of force as well as the many angles they form. A dancer moving on any one of these diagonals, aware of the powerful bisecting points of other diagonals, cannot help but acquire some of the strength inherent in such

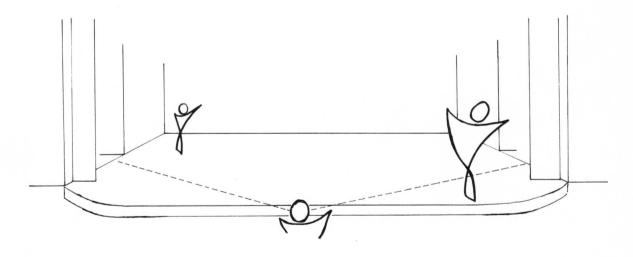

a perspective. Certainly an awareness of its existence may be used as a potential source of dramatic tension.

The position of the audience determines the relative directions of forward, backward, sideward, and diagonal. As the dancer moves *forward*, toward the audience, his figure becomes larger, more direct, and obvious, simply as a result of perspective. As he moves *backward*, away from the audience, he appears smaller, impersonal, and usually less important.

As he moves to the *side*, across the performance area, he presents a changing view of his figure. The design seems two dimensional and flat, and only the dancer's body has the potential for sculptured roundness. After his figure crosses center stage, it becomes less important, unless it is strengthened by the bold frame verticals of a box stage.

As he moves *diagonally* forward across the performing area, he gains the combined strength of the powerful diagonal plus the increasing apparent size of his figure, with its more rounded aspect. This creates the appearance of "becoming" and evokes a sense of affirmation. It is decorative as well, in the appearance of the vertical body line and the diagonal as they bisect.

When diagonals are combined into zigzags, the audience sees lines that seem to jab at space and then repeat themselves at another angle. These appear broken, changeable, and indecisive.

When lines of equal length repeat at right angles, the resulting *square* appears to enclose a space, to set up a controlled routine of repetition.

There is a wide potential of straight-line combinations—from geometric figures to countless irregular variations on a straight line. The combinations of side, forward, backward, and oblique all acquire some of the characteristics of each element involved. Because of the performance area, any straight line described by the dancer's body necessarily ends somewhere within the stage space before a new straight line begins.

In addition to straight-line paths, there are equally versatile curving lines. Undoubtedly the most complete curved line is a *circle*, with its projection of smooth ongoingness. Here the dancer could continue indefinitely on this path and still remain within the performance area.

A circle doubled in the opposite direction results in a *figure-eight*, which adds contrast and design interest to the structure of dance movement.

Scallops, or partial circles, are lyrical in form; they exaggerate points of beginning and ending.

The dramatic implications of the *spiral*, with its encircling or ever-widening form, depend on the point of beginning and the scope and direction of its path.

There are many combinations that can be developed by simply extending a curved line, each new element yielding its particular character to the over-all pattern. There is an even wider potential for spatial design in combinations of straight and curved lines. In fact, everything that moves will follow either one, the other, or both!

SPACE:
THE
CIRCULAR
STAGE

The choreographer who must deal with a circular stage must adapt movement patterns, such as those described above, to a much more problematic space. Most choreographers and critics do not consider dance equally interesting from all angles. They insist it should be viewed like a painting, from one direction and only one. There is no doubt that projection of dramatic intensity and linear design varies for different sections of the audience at a performance "in the round."

At such a performance, however, there is a greater emphasis upon the three-dimensional quality of the dancers. Perhaps the many objections to "dance in the round" are not so much that it should not be, but rather that it cannot exist without altering our concept of projection and design. Nonetheless, the formation of the early Greek chorus and the action circle of the primitives used dancers in the round. Despite such historical precedent, considerable readjustment seems to be required of choreographer, dancer,

and audience. Many aspects of dance have resisted change—
especially if they have long been accepted—until someone with
courage creates something new. Recognizing the problems of
circular staging is not enough; we must also recognize its potential
for a fresh look at dance.

It is important for a choreographer to keep in mind that designs in space are created not only by the dancer's body, but also
by the position of his arms, legs, head, shoulders, hips, and other

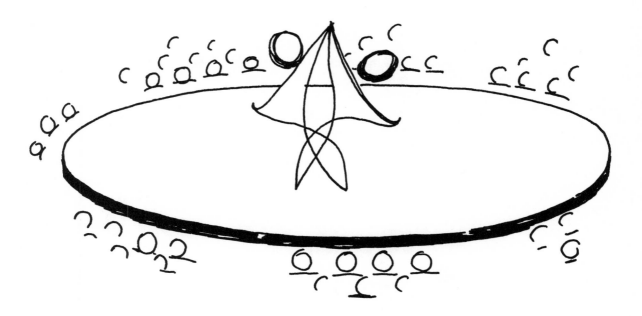

jointed parts. When more than one dancer is used, there are increasingly complex dynamic images produced by action and interaction between the dancers and the space of the performing area. Indeed, as one or many dancers move, they describe designs both on the floor and in space, even as if they were little black characters sweeping across a great expanse of white space. Dance, after all, is a language and an art form, and the choreographer, like the poet, uses his language to make a communication that is attractive as well as meaningful.

AND TIME

Dance uses energy to fill space, but it must do so within time. The elements of time include the factors of *tempo* and *rhythm,* which are of special concern to dancers. What is fast? What is slow? Only when some tempo is established can we identify one that is either faster or slower. Rhythm is a term that identifies a patterned relationship — sometimes a simple repetition and sometimes a complex development.

TIME: TEMPO

The tempo, or speed, of a dance is determined by the time span in which a given series of movements is completed, the period in which the dancer's body must accomplish a sequence of actions. Fast movement is usually more active and exciting; slow movement reduces the stimulation.

TIME: RHYTHM

Rhythm requires a structuring of movement patterns. There are a series of beginnings, developments, and endings leading to a rise, a bringing together, and a resolution. This structure may be compared to the rhythmic organization of music. The rhythm pattern comes into focus, is stressed, and is moved away from, in a clearly defined, planned sequence. Each transition, from beginning to middle and from middle to end, must be predetermined. Simple repetitions of stress and action evoke a feeling of regularity and balance; complex and obscure repetitions give rise to disturbance and excitement. Even random movement as dance requires planning to create the appearance of randomness.

How do energy, space, and time relate to the choreographer's purpose? We are concerned here with dance as an art form, in contemporary acceptance. "Contemporary" is, of course, a general term, but it may be taken to mean an approach to dance limited only by the movement capability and sensitivity of the performer, and the imagination, courage, and craft of the choreographer. Preformed movement patterns such as "steps," "routines," or "combinations" are not used. Rather, significant movement sequences are drawn out of human experience and the very act of moving. Form develops from the manipulation of these movements according to the dictates of the choreographer. While basic content may come from ancient as well as current sources, it is expressed primarily by the movement selected—colored by the character of the choreographer and performer, and unhampered by conventional ways of moving.

"Modern dance," historically, has been a breaker of rules. Classical ballet limited its choreographers to a movement code, but "dance" in contemporary terms means movement selected on the basis of its relevance to the human condition, movement which

will serve the purpose of an idea rather than merely act out a libretto or accompany a musical score. The choreographer in contemporary dance has freedom of choice and freedom of action. It is
through understanding and control of the factors of energy, space,
and time that this freedom is realized.

2
The End . . .
CHOREOGRAPHY

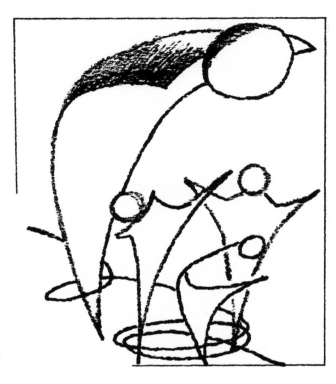

Choreography is choice and action. It is the process of selecting and forming movement into a dance. It is derived from the Greek: *choreia*, a choral dance; and *graphia*, writing. Literally, the word *choreography* implies the writing of group dance, but actually means designing the action, whether or not the design is written out. How-

19

ever, as dance is language, choreography is putting that language into form. A choreographer is a maker, a creator of dances. He seeks to create an expression by having dancers move according to his design. He manipulates movement to achieve his intent, even though he may find it hard to put this intent into words. Indeed, his choice of movement often serves a nonverbal purpose. Still, if he is unaware of any guiding premise, no matter how subtle, then he is improvising and has not yet started the actual designing of the dance. No matter how important unconscious motivation may be, a novice in any art needs to proceed on the basis of conscious intent. Exploration in movement is an important step in the choreographic process. It unleashes imagination and demands consideration and analysis of the relevance of movement to intent. But it is just a beginning, a point of departure for the process that ends in a completed expression of artistic purpose.

THE ROLE OF THE CHOREOGRAPHER

Choreography is obviously a creative act and, as such, somewhat mysterious. In a world where a premium is placed on objective, verifiable evidence, where methodology is cherished, the highly subjective and personal nature of creativity is a little frightening. The artistic process cannot be regimented; it does not allow shortcuts. There is no recipe for success; indeed, success itself is not clearly defined. Artistic endeavor is not a venture for the timid soul—it takes courage and stamina. And all too often dancers simply evade the whole issue.

"I need more skill in movement," one dancer says, and goes from studio to studio trying on the techniques offered. "Everyone knows that you must have good technical control of body movement before you can start choreographing dances." How much control? What will you do with your collection of techniques? "I'm not creative," another dancer insists, convinced that he can't choreograph like Humphrey or Tudor, so why bother? Of course it *is* easier and certainly more secure to follow directions than to start the tedious exploration and endless decision-making of the creative process. It is also less traumatic to collect a bag of movement tricks and to criticize the creativity of others! But everyone has a potential for creativity if he truly is willing to exercise it. Actually, choreography is a most exciting and rewarding process which every dancer should try.

"I don't know what to do, all of my ideas have been used," is another complaint. Nonetheless, many of the best dances come from simple and unpretentious ideas. One of the universal problems of beginning choreographers is an excessive regard for complex and socially significant proclamations, rather than uncluttered expressions that come out of personal experience.

Why should dancers bother with the difficult and time-consuming process of choreography? Of course, all dancers are not choreographers, nor should they be, any more than all musicians should be composers. While there is an ever-increasing call for skilled performers, there is an even greater demand for something more than mere technical skill. The dancer will be a more highly aware performer if he has experienced a choreographer's problems:

choice of relevant movement phrases out of a tangle of possible movement, identification of bases for choice of movement, consideration of and acquaintance with elements of design, dynamics, rhythm, and their interrelationships. The greatest problem in dance is not to train technicians, but to develop discriminating choreographers to provide something for technicians to perform.

It is often said that no one can tell anyone else how to write a poem, paint a picture, or choreograph a dance. Perhaps this is true. Certainly the final work of art represents a personal and lonely venture. But preliminary explorations to direct the beginner's efforts may cut down on some of the frustrating trial and error. An introduction to the basic aspects of energy with which to move, places to go, and when to get there may help to direct exploration. Let it be clear that these are simply tools for the beginning choreographer to work with, to be aware of, as he starts his personal search for movement that suits his purpose. The more he experiments, the more he will find. The more decisions he makes about movement, the more sensitivity he will develop.

CHOREOGRAPHY AND INDIVIDUALITY

Each choreographer is affected by his point of view as a person. He will often develop a system peculiar to his nature. Some identify the idea of a dance very clearly before they start; others first study accompaniment scores; still others improvise movement until an idea occurs to them. Some choreographers uncover a rhythmic structure and then build movement themes upon it; some need a literal story for a springboard; some seek kinetic images to develop. The proficient choreographer is not limited to any one of these approaches but will find varied avenues to creativity.

No matter what the process, all choreographers search for movement. Some of the movements they find will be kept, others rejected. Important movement themes must be developed, and sequential action must be formed out of decisions as to the relevance or irrelevance of basic materials. What is done with these materials, how they develop, depends largely upon the choreographer concerned—his experience, imagination, courage, and above all, what he wishes to express.

THE CHOREOGRAPHIC PROCESS

Choreographers, as all other creators in the arts, are concerned with *content, form, technique,* and *projection.* These words describe particular aspects of the choreographic process; all of them are necessarily present, but any one of them may be given more or less emphasis, depending upon the choreographer's intent.

Content refers to the underlying significance, the central concern of the work. This may be verbally identifiable or it may be inexpressible in words. But the content must result from the choreographer's intention. It is the effect that the choreographer is attempting to promote that will direct the selection of movement, control its organization, govern its form, and modify its action.

ASPECTS OF THE PROCESS: CONTENT

Form is the shape, the sequence, the organization of the action. After the initiation of the movement theme, something must happen. One movement phrase is followed by another, sometimes varied, contrasted, or developed. There may be theme and countertheme, rhythmic complications, or a dynamic resolutior But

ASPECTS OF THE PROCESS: FORM

certain action *belongs* in certain places, and it is the choreographer's task to determine where.

Sometimes it appears that form can only result from an analysis of intent, that the action must grow out of a logical sequence controlled by the choreographer's purpose. But sometimes the action seems to find its own direction, like a poem that creates its own images and rhythms, that literally writes itself.

ASPECTS OF THE PROCESS: TECHNIQUE

Technique, like form, is a means to the end of communicated significance. Both form and technique are valuable as tools, often exciting to demonstrate and interesting to watch, but important only as an aid to projecting purpose. Obviously the dance with potentially excellent content cannot come into full performance if the form is vague or the technical ability of the dancer is inadequate.

It is equally true that magnificent technique and brilliant form cannot save a dance which lacks significance. However, there is a tendency on the part of most audiences to overlook the latter in spite of this shortcoming. It would appear that, "He did *nothing* well," is better than, "He did *something* poorly." It all depends upon the relative value placed upon these important aspects of the process.

Dance, like music, must be performed in order to come into being. After the choreographer or the composer completes the organization of his materials, he often provides a notated record of his work. Unfortunately, however, systems of movement notation are not used as frequently as musical notation. Dancers and choreographers often depend upon kinetic memory or personal hiero-

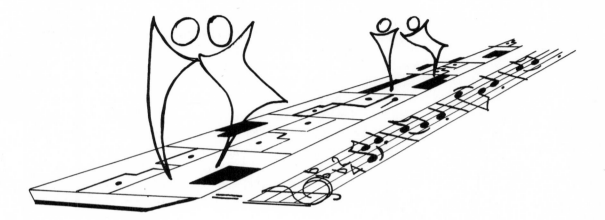

glyphics. Both the composer and choreographer turn the finished work over to sensitive and skilled performers, who devote extensive rehearsal time and deep personal involvement to re-create it in a finished performance. Ideally, the original creator assumes the role of director to oversee the execution of his work according to his original design.

Projection is controlled by the dancer-performer. It is that magic of rapport of the choreographer's plan with an audience's perception. While the form of the dance and the performer's technical ability are important, it is only when a bridge of communication between audience and performer is complete that dance comes to life. Sincerity, conviction, involvement, and discipline must blend with movement skill and a passionate concern for interpret-

ASPECTS OF THE PROCESS: PROJECTION

ing the choreographer's intent. It is when the choreographer's intent, selection of movement, and development of form, and the dancer's polished technical performance and dedicated projection are all accomplished that the cycle of creation is complete and the dance's meaning is communicated.

Expression in dance comes about as a result of the total act of moving – not because of any particular gesture, rhythmic trick, or good intention. The place where the dancer is, what he is doing, as well as how he is affecting the space around him, are all important. The rhythm, design, and dynamics are all consciously manipulated and controlled. Anything not important to the total expression is a distraction, and sometimes in our concern for *finding* movement we forget that we must also *get rid* of movement. Dance, as language, must be *formed* and then *edited* and *re-formed*.

It is difficult to talk or write about a dance, to reconstruct in words what has been designed in action, through movement sensation, idea, feeling, kinetic memory, and a host of connotations intermingled in the movement itself. As children grow and develop, they forget many of the movement-sensations they have had simply because they find no words to describe them. The language we know structures our experience. Nowhere is this more obvious than in the choreographer who is limited to what he can describe verbally. It is equally true of the viewer who is limited to verbal identifications.

One great task of the choreographer is to recognize the validity of the nonverbal and to be sensitive to the subtleties of movement that cannot be described in words. It is equally important to evade the trap of invariably associating certain movements with certain meanings. For example, "vertical movement implies heights and depths," "curved movement is always smooth and legato," "jagged movement is nervous and uncertain." When movement is so codified it loses its potential as a subtly expressive medium. This codification is similar to asserting that D minor in music is always anguish or that red in painting means excitement. Such responses are oversimplified and mechanical and are usually passed on by conditioning the young. Significance lies, rather, in an intricate web of relationships among all the elements concerned in a *specific* dance.

As the choreographer selects his compositional material, he draws from his own perceptions and remembrances. He examines his feelings, prejudices, and convictions, and from them he formulates his own images. In brief, he transforms his own perception of reality, with the possible exception of instances where he may deliberately copy the outward aspects of some "realistic" form. Various stylistic approaches to composition have come to be associated with schools or groups, each defined by its own characteristic way of perceiving reality.

STYLISTIC APPROACHES

Realism is an attempt to reproduce the appearance of "things as they are." But realistic approaches may vary, and interpretations of reality are not the same as actual photographs of it. Although an artist may strive for a duplication of the actual, his work will nonetheless be a projection of his personality, limited by his time and place. Realism, in other words, does not eliminate the artist's need to consider his selection of material.

Expressionism is an attempt to project the artist's emotional approximation of or intensification of reality. No attempt is made to copy reality; the emphasis is upon creating the personal expression of the real.

Impressionism is concerned with suggestion, with an oblique look at reality, as if through a cloud or mist. In this style it is usual

Realism   *Expressionism*

to exaggerate a segment of reality in order to highlight the artist's comment.

In cubism there is a surprising arrangement of forms in both space and time. One has the feeling that all forms are transparent and that reality can therefore be seen from all sides at once. One can see the front, back, sides, top, and bottom from the same van-

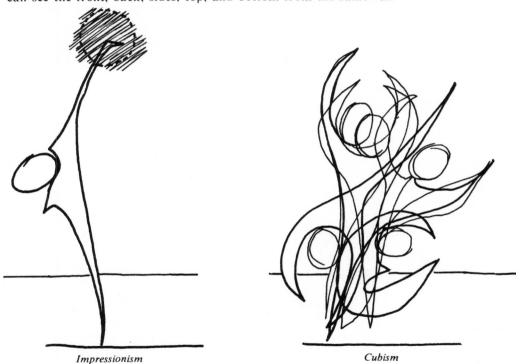

Impressionism   *Cubism*

tage point, entirely upsetting traditional perspective. While this is particularly pointed in the graphic arts, it is applicable to dance as well. The artist is sharing a remarkable and extraordinary view of reality as he sees it. This point of view is disturbing to some people because of the obvious excursion from "things as they are."

The surrealists also have a distorted view of reality and tend to disassociate forms from their ordinary setting and time. They seize an image and dart off into the unknown. Fish may walk down a busy street or watches melt over billowing clouds. The result often seems illogical, fragmented, and dreamlike as materials gravitate into unlikely and absurd relationships.

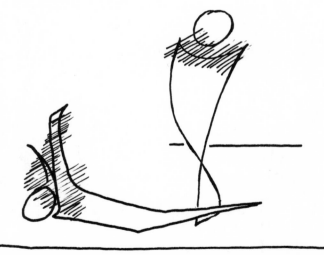

Surrealism

Whatever the approach to organizing content into a form, principles of *abstraction* and *distortion* are used. Both have been used through the centuries in all of the arts. They are merely means of expression and do not, as is commonly believed, indicate an absence of meaning. Abstraction is here defined as the essence, the core, the very heart of reality. The abstraction of climbing, for example, is that movement which is most central to the act and without which the act is something else. The abstraction of anger, in dance, is that brief movement which conveys the basic emotion simply and clearly, unmixed with suggestions of fear, disgust, or some other feeling. The process of abstraction is the paring away of *everything* save elemental characteristics; reducing something to its most essential identity. Distortion, as a means of treating the materials of expression, means any deviation or extension from the natural. This may progress by subtraction from the reality of a thing or by adding something to the reality that was not there before.

PRINCIPLES: ABSTRACTION

PRINCIPLES: DISTORTION

The view taken of reality and the methods employed to form the expression are entirely at the discretion of the choreographer. It often takes great courage to follow the dictates of a creative act, especially when it seems so much easier to add one movement to another and to come up with what many will call "a dance."

MEANING THROUGH MOVEMENT

In all of human life there is no more personal yet universal activity than movement. It is so much a part of being alive that we tend to take it for granted. Some movement is unconsciously controlled and may serve such physiological and psychological needs as reducing tension, balancing pressures, evading pain, or striking out at danger. Other movement, like the carefree skip of a child or the scrawl of a doodle, is random, and seemingly just happens. Much of our movement is carefully directed and serves a functional purpose—making or destroying, getting or evading, throwing or clutching, hitting or hugging.

The functional movement that provides food, shelter, and most belongings is called *work*. Equally functional to its different goals of recreation, socialization, and competition is *play*. Another kind of functional movement is to be found in the arts, where the artist directs his action to the forming of personal images in order to communicate an idea to his fellows.

In no art is movement more basic to expression than in dance, in which the instrument *for* expression is the moving body, and the materials *of* expression are patterned movements. Movement is the language which is formed into patterns.

All movement shows some evidence of form, even if the pattern is a precarious one, shaped by uncertainty. In the movement of work, form is determined by the function of the work; in the movement of play, form is determined by the object of the play. In dance, form is determined by the purpose of the choreographer.

MEANING:
FORM
AND
CONTENT

Dancers wage a continual controversy about the relative merits of form and content. One extreme position finds form all-important; the other extreme favors content as primary and insists that content creates its own form. The choice between the two is like the choice of whether to take food or water to a desert island. Each is important, and either is of little use without the other. However, both form and content may be interpreted in many ways; it is often hard to discern the point at which the meanings overlap. Personal prejudices and connotations become involved. The verbalizations used to justify a dogmatic choice are reminiscent of Humpty Dumpty's remarks in Lewis Carroll's *Through the Looking-Glass:* "When *I* use a word it means just what I choose it to mean — nothing more nor less." Form serves to clarify intent; form by itself is meaningless. Content is not clear unless its means are planned and organized. The two are inevitably interrelated.

In general, form is the relationship of movements which make up the shape of the dance. While the form may be recognizable in terms of a traditional or preconceived sequence, it may also be one that has never before been experienced. Because musicians have had a traditional and widely accepted record of form, we tend to borrow both terminology and structure from them. Sequential forms such as AB, ABA, rondo, theme and variation, suite, and sonata are aids in identifying relationships. It is true that these logical manipulations of one, two, or more themes are fundamental; many dances resolve into such sequence either by accident or design.

But when dance form does not follow any known structure it does not necessarily follow that form is lacking, but rather that *another* form has developed. Some organization is necessary, for its lack (however indiscernible it may be) would result in chaos. Even if the object of the dance were "randomness," it would be necessary to make some plan to create the appearance of randomness and to enable the dance to be repeated.

Should the beginning choreographer start with an idea, with some identifiable content, and then find the movement, or should he work from a movement and then discover an idea? I'm sure that many readers will feel strongly one way or another, but in my experience it doesn't really matter. What is important is that the movement that is finally selected is motivated and has some reason for being.

Some of the suggestions that follow were derived from *content*, from ideational sources; others are directed movement experiences based upon *form*, or structure of events. Another category includes movement based upon neither, but upon stimuli which represent an avenue for improvisations, unencumbered by planning.

There is one final comment to be made about these suggestions for action. The dancer's first impulse is often to mimic or *be* the thing suggested. This is a characteristic response of children, who have a wonderful belief in their ability, as the song says, to "Be a tree, be a sled, be a purple spool of thread." This method often insures a magical sincerity of action that mature artists strive to recapture. But an artist's response should be more creative. Hopefully including the conviction of the child, he should be concerned with man's relationship *to* rather than imitation *of* the stimulus.

Remember, we are human beings and operate in human ways. Rather than trying to *be* a tree, let us consider how a human being relates to a tree. It is something to lean against, to walk around, to

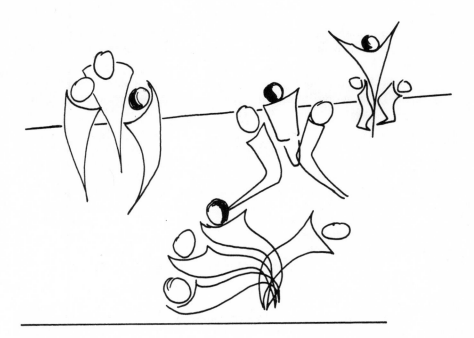

chop down and shave into splinters, to fly through, to hang orna-
ments on, to carve initials in, or to imagine as part of a great rain
forest. Rather than trying to *be* a stone, let us see how human beings
and stones are related. Stones are perhaps to stumble against, to
hurl, to pile up into a castle, to roll up a mountain as did Sisyphus,
to fit into a mosaic, to hang around a donkey's neck, or even to
cause us to imagine where the first stone came from.

The unique problem in creative forming of dance is in selecting image-provoking movements. This is not just to be thought
about or dreamed of, but must be pulled out of the action of the
human body.

The following springboards may serve as a start in exploration
for fresh action. Each will suggest a dozen more ways. As Santayana said:

> "Perceptions do not remain in the mind, as would be suggested
> by the trite simile of the seal and the wax, passive and change-
> less, until time wears off their rough edges and makes them
> fade. No, perceptions fall into the brain rather as seeds into a
> furrowed field or even as sparks into a keg of gunpowder.
> Each image breeds a hundred more, sometimes slowly and
> subterraneously, sometimes (as when a passionate train is
> started) with a sudden burst of fancy."—Quoted in John
> Dewey, *Art as Experience* (New York: Minton, Balch & Co.,
> 1934), p. 156.

EXPLORATIONS

Based upon content: ideational

Direct perceptions:
  Storm at sea
  Sound of laughter
  Children at play
  Starry sky

    City street
    Rocking chair
    Bargain counter
    Rush hour on the freeway
    The horizon
    Steaming pie

Kinaesthetic sensations:
    Tension to relaxation
    How it feels to run fast
    Pounding a nail
    Whipping cream
    Blowing up a balloon
    "Sitting on top of the world"
    Sailing in a strong wind
    Walking in outer space
    Riding on the tail of a kite

Sense-memory experiences (try to remember how it felt and
  relive it):
    On a sticky, hot day
    Locked in a small, dark room
    Late at night in a strange and dismal place
    The feel of sandpaper
    Taking a cold shower
    Tasting a sour lemon
    Hot sand on your feet

EXPLORATIONS:
IDEATIONAL

Skiing down a deep snow slope
Wind blowing from a mountain meadow
Diving into cool, green water

Natural action and gesture:
Human and animal locomotion
Bird in flight

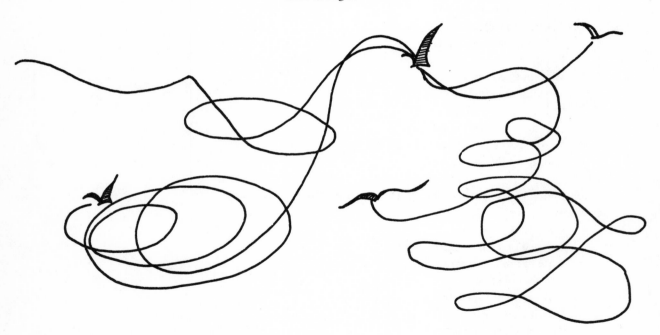

Rooster crowing
Workman at a lathe
Leopard crouching
Boy on a skateboard
Snake coiling
Woman scrubbing steps
Parachute jumper
Tennis players

First reaction in dramatic situations:
You trump your partner's ace
Hurricane warning is posted
You win $50,000 prize
Messenger brings black-edged letter
House is on fire
Earthquake is beginning
You got an A in physics
War is declared
Your leg is broken
The wedding date is set

Stereotyped gesture of:
Youth and old age
Boredom and concentration
Breathing
Obesity
Sleepwalking

EXPLORATIONS:
IDEATIONAL

Mob leader
Tightrope walker
Adolescent
Politician

Familiar movements done or observed:
    Class techniques
    Sports action
    Circus or television acts
    Movement habits of friends
    Traditional patterns of movement
        Folk dance
        Ethnic dance
        Current dance (social)
    Work movement
    Action of machines and gadgets

Social relationships:
    Warden and escaped convict
    King and peasant
    Father and son
    Sergeant and private
    Newsman and politician
    Lawyer and client
    Doctor and patient
    Teacher and pupil

Response to action words:
  Melt
  Wiggle
  Bounce
  Ooze
  Collapse
  Soar
  Snatch
  Cling
  "Gimme"
  Flip
  Jiggle
  Pitter-pat
  Slink

Function, shape, and feel of things around us:
  Ashtray
  Chewing gum
  Molasses
  Electric toaster
  Glue
  Picket fence
  Pillow
  Postage stamp
  Bean bag
  Pencil

Historical, legendary, or literary events or figures:
 Boston Tea Party
 Carrie Nation
 Pandora
 Davy Crockett
 United Nations Council meeting
 Paul Bunyan
 Athena
 Paul Revere
 Burning of St. Joan

Current topics, comics, headlines, TV, commercials:
 Another bank robbery
 Death to the dictator
 Where are you, Charlie Brown?
 Esteban to fight bulls Sunday
 Mrs. Ohsobig leaves for islands today
 Wrong way on the freeway again!
 "Step out of your shower feeling cleaner than ever"
 "How does she stay so sleek and slim?"
 Pow – Zowie – Wham, here's Batman!

Conversation to gossip:
 Develop a simple phrase in movement . . .
 Extend into a conversation with someone else . . .
 Break into gossip with several people . . .
 Then to a mob with all "talking" at once

Social rites:
    Initiation
    City council meeting
    First prom
    Revival meeting
    At the art gallery
    Wedding
    Funeral
    Tea party
    Strike
    Fourth of July celebration

Interpretation of subject matter:
    Poetry
    Biography
    Painting
    Music
    Sculpture
    Architecture
    Mobiles
    Conversations overheard
    Signboards
    Telephone directory
    Dictionary
    Etiquette book
    College catalog
    Vehicle code book

Based upon form: structural

Design and spatial relationships:
 Changes in
   Direction
   Level
   Size
   (With resulting patterns both in floor space and space
     around the dancer's body)
   Movement in one place
   Movement through space
   Combinations of these

Time relationships:
   Even and uneven rhythms
   Simple and complex rhythms
   Cumulative rhythm
   Resultant patterns
   Syncopation
   Mixed meter
   Canon
   Fugue
   Speed changes
   Rubato

Variations in use of energy:
  Changes in
      Intensity
      Quality
      Accent

Within space limitations:
  In a small square
  In a three-foot circle
  By a rope stretched diagonally between two pillars
  Around a single pylon
  Behind a screen
  On a high box
  By a rope suspended from the ceiling
  Surrounded by three benches
  By a stepladder in a corner
  Using both stage and audience space

Within time limitations:
  Thirty seconds
  Twelve-count phrase
  Reverberation of one gong tone
  Time of a spoken phrase
  Time it takes to spell your name
  Time of a musical phrase

**EXPLORATIONS:
STRUCTURAL**

New relationships among dancers:

In groups of two

Move with arms clasped, arms interlocked, feet held together, and shoulders touching

Use each of these relationships in one place and through space

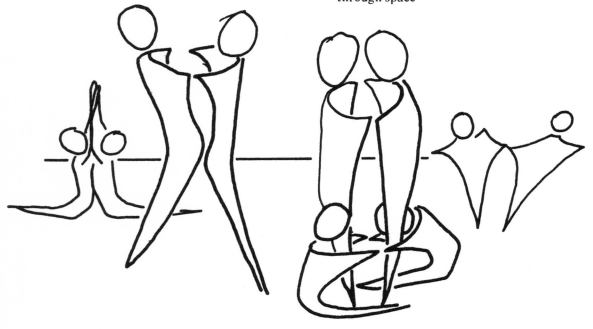

In groups of three
   Hold hands, then
      Skip
      Run
      Hop
      Fall
      Crawl

Question and answer:
   Solo or group
      Initiate a movement
      Self or others respond by
         Mirroring
         Contrasting
         Extending
         Reversing

Relation to inanimate object:
   Move toward
   Away
   Around
   Over
   Under
   Through
   From bottom to top
   As if it were not there

EXPLORATIONS:
STRUCTURAL

Relation to other dancers:
   Move toward
   Away
   Around
   Over
   Under
   Through
   With
   In opposition
   In contrast
   As if they were not there

Extremes and contrasts:
   Overstatement and understatement
   Exaggerated contrasts
      Large–small
      High–low
      Loud–soft
      Fast–slow
      Sticky–fluffy
      Tight–loose
      Straight–curved
      Still–active
      Smooth–jerky
      Flat–sharp

Simple manipulation of theme:
    Choose a simple four-count theme . . .
    Repeat it . . .
    Develop into a seven-count phrase . . .
    Repeat original four-count . . .
    Contrast with a new four-count . . .
    Return to original four-count movement

Simple manipulation of three groups of dancers:
    All perform the same movement traveling forward and backward . . .
    Group 1 continues original action; group 2 starts in opposite direction; group 3 does action in one place . . .
    Group 1 moves from right to left; groups 2 and 3 do action in one place . . .
    Group 1 moves diagonally forward; group 2 encircles group 1; group 3 encircles group 2 . . .
    All repeat action of first statement

Simple time manipulation with two groups of dancers:
    All perform the same nine-count movement phrase simultaneously, moving in a circle for five counts, in a straight line for four counts . . .
    Group 1 continues as before, repeating several times
    Group 2 waits for five counts, then starts and continues several times

AB

> Develop a movement theme for circles or dots . . .
>
> Develop another movement theme for squares or dashes . . .
>
> Perform in sequence as "Squaring the Circle" or "Dots and Dashes"

ABA

> Choose an axial movement phrase and develop a theme to be called "In One Place" . . .
>
> Choose some locomotor movement and develop a theme to be called "Through Space" . . .
>
> Perform "In One Place," "Through Space," and finish with repetition of "In One Place"

Variations on a theme:

> Form a simple movement theme and rehearse it carefully so that you are sure of its components . . .
>
> Vary this selected movement phrase in at least five different ways (experiment with varying relationships of space, time, and dynamics) . . .
>
> Develop another and contrasting theme and make variations on this

IMPROVISATIONS

Chance discovery of movement:

> Move from one place to another and another

Accompany yourself with sounds you can make by yourself
Experiment with points of compass, i.e., north, north by
east, north northeast, northeast by north, northeast,
northeast by east, east by north, etc.
Follow pattern of light or grain of wood in floor

Isolated action of body parts:
From isolated stationary position and then while travel-
ing through space, move
One arm
Head
Hips
One leg
One hand
Shoulder
Fingers
Elbow

Jam session:
Rotate leaders for group participation in exploration and
identification of a simple movement sequence
or
Given a simple locomotor theme, each leader changes just
one thing and continues leading group through space
until everyone is performing it, then leaders change
for another variation of the original sequence

IMPROVISATIONS
With sets, props, and costume bits:

    Stool
    Eggbeater
    Ball
    Rope
    Stepladder
    Open door frame
    Hat or cape
    Feather
    Two yards of tubular jersey
    Ball of yarn
    Metronome
    Square of tulle
    Length of elastic

Magic circle:

    Dancers sit on the floor in a circle, clapping an under beat . . .
    One or two dancers move on inside of circle . . .
    Each chooses one to take his place by encircling an individual

Part and whole:

    Eye focuses on a place and body moves to that place
    Another body part initiates impulse and entire body moves (static and locomotor)

Alternatives by lot:
>   Construct a set of pairs of cards on which are indicated such choices as:
>>   Start in center–enter from left
>>   Smooth, free action–tight, restricted action
>>   Curved and curling–angular patterns
>>   Slow fall–twenty seconds inactivity
>   Choose one of each pair as a directive to action

With self-accompaniment:
>   Sit and play a noisemaker or simple instrument
>   Start moving with it, using accompaniment as a part of action

With materials:
>   Twist wire into shapes
>   Manipulate paper, ribbon, fish net, or cardboard
>   Using water-based paint, apply designs on sets, suspended butcher paper, dancers' bodies, floor
>   Read section from large dictionary, move to someone else and pass it on

See it, do it . . . do it, see it:
>   With a sketch pad and felt-pen, doodle three or four simple designs, then move according to these designs
>   Reverse the process; move first and then sketch the patterns of movement

IMPROVISATIONS   Balance to off-balance:

                  Sit on a box and find point of best balance . . .

                  Slowly move until you lose your point of balance . . .

                  Return to balanced position in some different way . . .

                  Repeat above from a standing position . . .

                  Repeat above from a moving pattern

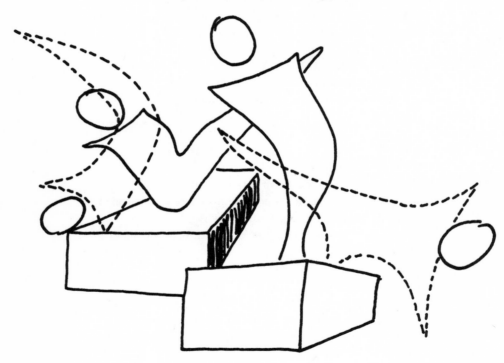

Pick a number:

> Pick a number from two to ten, clap a rhythmic pattern using the number as the underlying beat, then move in this rhythmic pattern

Somebody tell:

> In groups of three dancers, one calls direction and others respond in movement, for example, "Circles, whee, no-no-no, hoppity, anything goes"

Speak-do:

> Select one word (e.g., "where") and say it three different ways . . .
>
> Do the same with one simple gesture and perform it in three ways . . .
>
> Put the chosen word into a simple sentence, e.g., "Where in the world am I?" . . .
>
> Do the same thing with the gesture

So what:

> Invent a simple movement phrase . . .
>
> Develop it to a point of no return . . .
>
> Then make something drastic happen to it

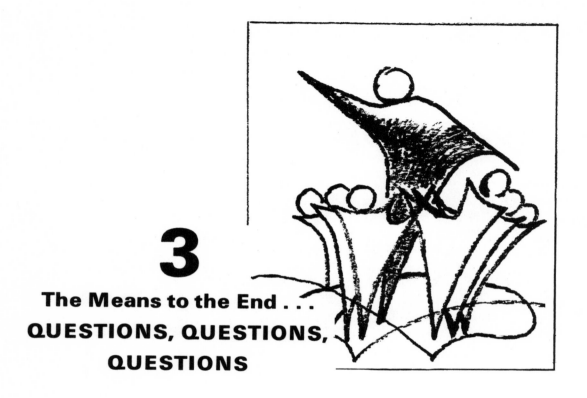

3

The Means to the End . . .
QUESTIONS, QUESTIONS, QUESTIONS

Watching an experienced choreographer yields fascination and wonder, but few clues on how to compose a dance. Yet the most versatile choreographer had to start somewhere and find his way alone. How many hours were spent choosing and deleting, manipulating movement, and changing rhythm, dynamics, and spatial design? How long did it take to discover the inevitable action, to pare away all super-fluous material? When could he finally say to himself: "The dance is complete"?

"WHAT MOVEMENT SHALL I USE?"

The first and most basic question that a potential choreog-rapher asks is, "What movement shall I use?" Unfortunately, what usually happens is that action is selected from previous dance ex-perience—bits of technique, favorite movements, or remembered patterns—joined together like assorted beads on a string. This is only rearrangement, not fresh and creative formulation.

To find a basic movement you must first move, not merely physically or emotionally or intellectually or even dramatically, but as a total human being. Within this total act of movement lies the seed of the dance form. A purpose to guide the form may come before the movement or out of it; in either case, the movement must be carefully examined and analyzed. It is often chosen from "real life": from representational gestures, current happenings, or rec-ollections of things seen, heard, or done. Sometimes it is selected from the imagination, from something "dreamed up." It may be contrived from an idea, sensation, or feeling, quite unrelated to outer reality.

The decision as to whether the movement selected is destined as the primary theme or as a means to establishing a mood or as simply one part of the whole is yet to be made. It is, so far, merely something to work with. Usually the movement selected will need clarification and reworking, or on occasion, if the choreographer is sensitive and really brave, it may be discarded for a new theme. The selectivity of the choreographer depends upon his concern with perfecting his expression—whether it must be "just so" or just another movement.

The very process of selecting *some* movement out of many possible movements is in itself a primary act of creativity. The basis for such a choice is highly personal, because it is a means toward the expression to be made—which is in part *self-* expression or, more precisely, expression *through* self. Let us be quite clear, choreographic expression is not an explosion of symptoms of how one feels . . . like a child having a temper tantrum. Choreography as expression is not *having* a tantrum as such, with all its uncontrolled aspects, but *forming* a temper tantrum.

Basically, the choreographer chooses a movement as a result of identifying something within the act of movement itself. It may

be a "jagged" or "spiraled" action or a gesture of work or play. It may be from a folk or period piece or derived from a literal or musical theme. It may be an action that resists verbalization, that is readily identifiable only as "this movement." But it always gives promise of conveying the choreographer's purpose, the content of the dance, and it always holds possibilities of development into a dance form, the eventual structure of the work.

If the choreographer is seriously concerned with movement choices, then he must be prepared to lavish time, effort, and concentration on the relative merits of possible movements. Far more important than finding *a* movement is the decision-making required for finding *the* movement—*the* movement that truly promotes the sense of the dance.

"WHERE DOES MOVEMENT COME FROM?"

Movement is the most persistent experience in living—the first and last expression of life. It has both objective and subjective characteristics and significances. Sometimes movement denotes particular purpose; sometimes it seems random and unstructured. In any instance, it is beset with innumerable connotations. Purposeful and universally recognizable movement patterns give reality to dance material. Such patterns grow out of the primal motives of man: love, hate, hope, fear, aspiration, greed, and simple animal joy. In these emotions are the seeds of gesture common to most people, the postural stereotypes, the natural responses. Another source of movement is the sum of conventional gestures common to a place and time. For instance, contemporary American audiences recognize an extended forefinger as a gesture of pointing, but Germans extend both arm and forefinger, and the British sometimes use the chin for this purpose. The meaning of such a gesture comes from the viewers' experience. Although such meaning may be widely recognized and quite useful to a choreographer, it is not universal.

But in any movement, even one that offers clear-cut identification of a common emotion, there are slippery, hard-to-trace overtones. These are the human, the personal, the idiosyncratic variables that slide from the grasp. It is in these nebulous areas that the symbolic and dramatic "stuff" of choreography lies. Although we may discover movement for dance in a variety of life experiences, there is usually a high degree of resistance to any such movement that does not fit preconceived ideas of what dance should be.

There is an almost pathological tendency in a beginning choreographer to assemble bits of stereotyped action with little regard for anything except: "Here is a good movement!" The problem arises, in part, because there are so few objective criteria for judgment. The rightness of a movement is partly a matter of personal opinion, preference, and decision. It is thus sometimes difficult to differentiate between the serious composition that is the artist's created illusion and the childish action that shows only the symptoms of the dancer's feelings. Yet the difference is crucial, for dance as an art must reflect discipline and an imaginative use of materials—not merely a collection of clichés or tricks.

Movement comes from a deliberate decision of the choreographer, who finally says: "This is the movement theme that I want to use." Initially, the action may have grown out of a natural movement, a mimed gesture, a stereotyped act, a literal interpretation, a dramatic image, a mood feeling, an exploration of time-space-force, or an apparently accidental movement that "just happened." Undoubtedly, the nature of the choice mirrors the choreographer's breadth of vision and experience, and the degree of his imagination and his involvement with the problem will greatly affect the results.

"WHAT SHALL I DO WITH THE MOVEMENT?"

There is no single way to choreograph a dance – the process is unique to each dance and extends from the choreographer's personality. Let it be remembered that while choreography is a *forming* of expression, it is never a *mold* for it. The choreographer is designing a fresh look at reality; he is intensifying and pointing out new relationships. In a way he is like an ardent photographer standing on a tall ladder, with his multiple telescopic lens pointed at an odd angle, through a fine mesh screen, searching for a new perspective on a blade of grass.

Hence there is no quick answer to the question, "What shall I do with the movement?" There are only more questions. What do you want to do with it? What do you have to say? What is your motivation? Will it serve your purpose to: repeat it, vary it, reinforce it, make fun of it, change its mood, caricature it, extend it, divide it into parts, develop it into a sequential form by introducing another theme, or throw it away and start all over?

The movement belongs where you finally decide to put it. Your decision is made in terms of motive, experience, and discrimination. After trying it in relation to other movement themes it will become apparent that it belongs here rather than somewhere else. The desperate alternative is to put it anywhere and trust to your luck!

"HOW DO I GIVE THE DANCE FORM?"

Sometimes the dance seems to shape itself, but the choreographer is finally responsible for deciding upon the sequence of actions. A dance develops and changes as it grows. As Picasso said of painting, dance is a "sum of destructions not thought out beforehand."

If the choreographer seeks to inform in a literal sense, he must shape his materials in universally recognized ways and must limit fantasy and emotional overtones. Too often this results in a kind of "acting out" that stifles imagery. If the choreographer is to develop an expression—his expression—he must have the courage to follow his own intent into whatever realm it leads. When form moves away from the commonplace, from the readily discernible stereotype, there will always be those who say: "I wonder what he is dancing about . . . I don't understand it." Communication of content in dance is necessarily complex; the choreographer's intent, the performer's interpretation, and the audience's perception may not coincide.

The following are comments from student choreographers as they discuss how they shaped some of their dance studies and how they view the sources and the potentialities involved in the experience of forming a dance:

> "A dominant movement theme starts the dance and is repeated by a trio, a solo figure and then in a kind of three voice form with solo, trio and duo interaction. A series of variations accent different aspects of the major theme. As I think about it and see it developing it just looks like a lot of different ways of making a real important statement. I guess this is an experience in form, but all kinds of exciting ideas are coming out of it."

Obviously the first theme chosen by this student was considered very important; the repetitions and the increasingly complex variations reinforced the initial idea.

> "I got my idea from Mondrian's 'Broadway Boogie Woogie,' making my thematic statement out of contrasting space and rhythm design. I meant it to have a feeling of opposition, conflict and speed."

In this case the choreographer deliberately exaggerated different spatial and rhythmic patterns to highlight contradictions in design. In spite of the hard contrast between pairs of these patterns, there were moments when parts of other movement sequences came in to subdue the conflict. Criticism from other class members was unanimous in identifying "too many different movement patterns, a kind of clutter."

"The first theme I call 'Spiral Trio' for it has many encir-
clements for three dancers, ending with jabbing straight lines.
After a transition of punctuating jumps the dancers stop all
movement and seem frozen in place. Then the whole group
melts into a lyrical and legato theme that I think I will call
'For Nine.' "

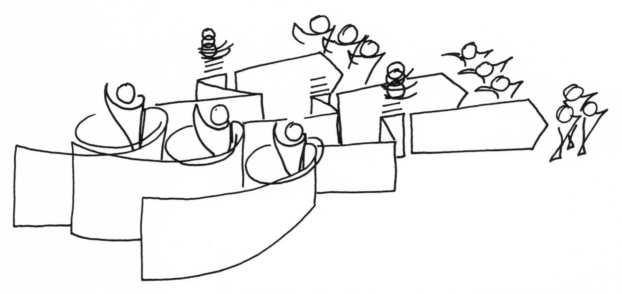

The shape of this dance was inevitable in terms of the dynamic
tension that developed from the first simple curve into the sharp
angles. The cessation of movement was almost electrifying; I feel

that it was an accident, but what a lucky accident! The resolution was a simple twelve-count theme performed intermittently by varying numbers of dancers, finally blending into a two-voice canon in which the unusual dynamic and spatial variables were explored.

> "There was a sentence in *The Lonely Crowd* that intrigued me, and I thought was a good idea for a dance. The line might be good for a program note: ' . . . etiquette is concerned not with encounters between individuals as such but with encounters between them as representatives of their carefully graded social roles.'
>
> "The dance starts with seven people wandering about and finally bumping into each other. Two dancers fall and three others climb over them. Two more dancers stand stiffly facing each other, almost as if they were going to fight. The next theme divides the group into two factions who start a bowing and ingratiating theme. This is all that I have. It's not that I don't have a lot of ideas and even movement, but it is so hard to decide which to use. I do think that the title 'Encounters' is appropriate."

This student was confronted with a typical problem of compromise. She was concerned that she should somehow keep the literal meaning and yet find a movement parallel that would not pantomime the action. It is possible that the sentence would have served best as a springboard to action, not as a mold for it.

One of the simplest questions for the choreographer to consider after choosing a movement theme is: "So what?" So you have a movement theme, what about it? What do you want to happen to it? What are the possibilities?

"WHERE DO I GO FROM HERE?"

Transitions, changing from one movement to another, are both a part of the theme that precedes and the theme that follows. Unless the choreographer wants a shock of unheralded differences, he should consider both the motivation of what has happened and the implication of what will happen. Introduction of something of the theme to come and repetition of some part of the theme that came before will, if nothing else, help an audience to recognize something as important enough to be presented more than once. One of the marks of good choreography is the smooth and carefully interwoven transition. Unless the dance calls for an obvious change, the audience should not be startled by one.

"DO MY CHOSEN MOVEMENTS PROJECT MY MEANING?"

It will never be possible to answer this question completely; the meanings of the dance will be interpreted in different ways by different people. The choreographer is fortunate if his work is responsible for generating even a general kinaesthetic response. As pointed out in the section titled, "Where Does Movement Come From?," some movement has universal meaning, and some has significance that belongs to the choreographer's time and place.

Both types of movement are comparable to representational painting, in which objects are widely or universally recognized. Other
movement is connotational, with overtones and implications that
are associated by the viewer with his own experiences and mem-

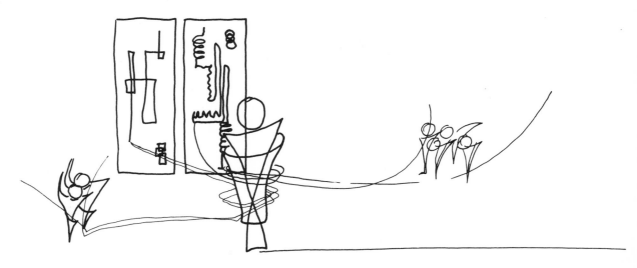

ories. Such movement is comparable to abstract painting, which
arouses a personal response in the viewer. According to his best
judgment, the choreographer chooses for his materials of expression those that seem most appropriate and relevant to him. To increase his understanding of the projection of meaning, he must
continue exploration, keep an open mind in analysis of the work,
and try to listen to qualified criticism.

Since dance comes into being only when it is performed, there is another variable to be considered. The choreographer needs technically proficient performers. In a parallel case a speaker needs to use a blend of precise words and clear syntax, well enunciated and phrased; he can lose a great idea by poor formulation and mumbling delivery. The same is true of dance and its medium of expression—movement. In fact, dancers with sensitivity and concern do more than follow a dance's form. They also enrich the projection designed by the choreographer. Ideally, the choreographer furnishes the movement design, indicates its purpose, and then assumes the dancers will be emotionally as well as technically able to communicate the significance of the work.

"WHAT'S IN A NAME?"

Sometimes significance can be conveyed in a title, for titles and, in some cases, program notes are a means of identifying a dance for both the choreographer and the observer. Sometimes a word or phrase will arise during the choreographic process. More often the choice of an inevitable and perfect title for the dance comes after an exhaustive search of words, even as final decisions are made about the movement. In any event, titles and program notes should develop out of the materials the choreographer is working with, and rather than describe the action, these words should excite a curiosity about it. In "Robe of Shadow," choreographed as a Master's thesis, Shizuko Iwamatsu used the following lines translated from an ancient Noh play:

" The sadness of autumn is infinite
 Voice of the wind and jabber of insects
 What tragic woman was I

 What tragic woman was I
 The autumn flowers wither
 The sounds of the insects fade
 The voice of the wind in the pines is lonely
 The sadness of autumn is infinite.''

As the dance uses movement to evoke a dynamic image, so the title may use a poetic image to give promise of what will come. The following titles illustrate this suggestive quality:

"Ruins and Visions"	Humphrey
"Dark Meadows"	Graham
"Dark Elegies"	Tudor
"Opus 51"	Weidman
"Root of an Unfocus"	Cunningham
"8 Clear Places"	Hawkins
"Totem"	Nikolais
"Acrobats of God"	Graham
"And Daddy Was a Fireman"	Weidman
"Village of Three"	Nikolais
"With My Red Fires"	Humphrey
"Pillar of Fire"	Tudor
"Here and Now with Watchers"	Hawkins
"Tossed as It Is Untroubled"	Cunningham

"HOW DO I KNOW IF IT'S ANY GOOD?"

Any artistic creation is evaluated in terms of personal reaction, colored by highly individualized concepts of value and adherence to those factors considered implicit in a work of art. There is such variation in audience response that a dance which moves one person may be quite uninteresting to another. But a really good dance *will* evoke some response from an audience, particularly if all aspects of design, performance, and production are complete.

There is no infallible formula guaranteeing that "This is a good dance; reproduce it for instant success." What is exciting and "right" in one dance will seem contrived and awkward in another. Predetermined concepts of unity, coherence, balance, harmony, and emphasis have only the significance that is attached to them. Each critic uses them to substantiate his own reaction. If some of these standards have reasonable meaning for you, aside from their traditional recitation value, then take them for your own. Your judgments will come out of your sense of value and discrimination, and will be affected by your concept of a work of art.

The only certain basis for the projection of a dance idea is dependence upon movement itself. Obviously the staging, lighting, sets, costumes, accompaniment, and technical performance are all important, but they are all secondary to movement.

Genius or novice, mature artist or amateur, you must choose movement on the basis of your best judgment. You will have succeeded in this if you become deeply involved in the problem of choice and find your way to an uncluttered and significant solution. It is your solution. Whether it is a satisfactory theatrical solution is another question. How do you really feel about the communicative powers of your dance? Are you willing to be responsible to a discerning audience? Will the critics agree with your solution and find yours a "good" dance? No matter how the dance is received, it will be a step on the way to the development of your standards of excellence.

Not everyone has equal interest, skill, or potential for the process of choreography. But anyone can find personal satisfaction, if not brilliant results, in the undertaking. Whatever is done will mirror the choreographer's philosophy of dance, art, and life. It will certainly make him more sensitive to other choreography and, perhaps, to the creative process.

Clearly the choreographer must be aware of his underlying convictions about art. If he believes that art should dazzle or simply entertain his audience, then he will seek movement to display the technical virtuosity or rhythmic complexity that does this. If he considers art as a representation of beauty, grace, and harmony in his world, then he will stress the grace and flow of pleasing and natural movement. If he believes art to be an abstraction or distortion of the natural, then he will search for imaginative ways to convey such a modification of nature.

The atmosphere for choreography must be permissive. The choreographer must be free to find his own way or to perpetuate someone else's method. Only by experimentation, by discovering a personal framework of values, can he develop a really creative dance composition. And there must be time—time for discovering, trying, rejecting, and again finding movement. There must be time for the incubation of ideas. Any dancer can solve movement puzzles and come up with pat answers to movement-exercise problems. But a real concern for the *best possible* solution as a *creative act* is something else. It cannot be stressed too often that this takes time, effort, patience, and involvement.

4

The Elements of the Art . . .
SOME ABC'S FOR
CHOREOGRAPHERS

One of the marks of choreography as an art form is the choreographer's approach to the selection and organization of movement. Rather than merely rearranging some preformed actions, he develops each movement phrase as a fresh and new statement, as if it were happening for the first time. The choreographer, as artist, has an individual vision, sees new relationships, provokes uncommon images, and, with a maximum of disciplined control of his materials, forms movement into a dance where before there was only random, functional, or play movement. He is creative.

"Creative" is an overworked word. It has been applied to almost every conceivable activity and product. It has been considered an intuitive faculty, an extension of intelligence, an hereditary tendency, or even a visitation of the muses. It has been defined as a basic urge, common to all human beings, and as a rare capacity, possessed by only a happy few.

How much does "creativity" as it takes place in the process of choreography rely upon intuition? There is usually a period of conscious exploration with bits of movement, an extension of these into longer sequences, additions and deletions, and a search for an inevitable development of movement phrases. There is usually a careful consideration of the dynamic patterning – of where each movement goes and when it arrives. Sometimes there seems to be a flash of insight, but more often there is a relentless shaping and reshaping – the throwing away of one movement and the finding of another – until a movement sequence that suits the choreographer evolves. Perhaps intuition operates more frequently than this description allows, but it is well for a beginning choreographer to examine his insights carefully. It might be said of creativity what has been said of genius: "It is the capacity for taking infinite pains."

A number of traits are said to characterize the behavior of creative people. They would be valuable to any choreographer:

Originality, curiosity, and resourcefulness
Fluency in ideas and images
Involvement and motivation, to the point of obsession
Sensitivity, taste, and the strength to resist stereotypes
Discrimination and the courage to reject the unnecessary
Skill, endurance, and perserverance
Faith in personal decisions
Capacity for critical evaluation

The trait of curiosity deserves special emphasis. Assuming that you feel involvement and motivation, nothing can prove more valuable to you than a willingness to experiment and explore— both with ideas and movement. But before you begin, examine the goal you have in view.

Is it to solve a class problem? Class experimentations in exploration and composition serve to stimulate the ingenuity of students in a number of ways. Don't simply solve a problem in any way in order to satisfy a requirement. Creative people care; they work for themselves. The problem offers an opportunity to increase your sense of discrimination and to broaden your grasp of the tools of composition. Try to use many approaches to the problem to increase your understanding of the process of choreography.

GOALS: PROBLEM SOLVING

Do you want to provide a vehicle for your technical skill? Skill in movement is a priceless asset, to be developed and used for freeing the dancer to fulfill the purpose of the dance, but not as a structuring mold into which all dances must be fitted. Think of technique as a *means* to an end, not as an end in itself.

GOALS: TECHNICAL SKILL

GOALS:
PERSONALITY
EXHIBITION

Do you need an outlet for exhibiting your personality? Because of the personal nature of both choreography and performance, the choreographer's personality will be evident, but not merely as testimony of *how* he feels. Dance as art is not a direct expression of the inner self. Rather, it is a disciplined form that is made public and possible through that self. Exhibitions of personality, sometimes called "self-expression," are best practiced behind closed doors or in therapy!

GOALS:
STORY
TELLING

Would you like, literally (and literarily), to tell a story? If the literal or factual message is most important, try speaking the words that tell the story. What then can movement add to further this meaning? Perhaps the literal meaning should serve only as a springboard to a different kind of expression in movement.

GOALS:
MUSICAL
INTERPRETATION

Do you crave to give your interpretation of music? Many dancers feel comfortable with the security of musical form, especially if they like the music. Often it is said to be "just right to *dance to*." (One is mindful of portly ladies in togas, swaying in "interpretive dance.") Music has a medium and a form of its own; it is composed to be heard. Upon what basis do dancers assume an ability to interpret what is already complete in another medium? Of course there is no regulation that limits the use of music, but it must be recognized that the already completed form of the music will necessarily dominate any dance interpretation. In such cases, the music is not really an accompaniment for the dance. Rather, the dance is an accompaniment for the music.

GOALS:
ENTERTAINMENT

Do you wish to entertain an audience, to be a performer? An audience that comes, much less pays, to see a dance concert should be accorded due respect and consideration. Frantic "making-up-a-dance-for-the-concert" projects may be exhilarating experiences for beginning choreographers and dancers, but the audience is not always equally fascinated. Without experience, discrimination, and taste—all of which come only with great effort over a long period of time—student performances are usually best seen in less formal settings. A demonstration or an informal studio program or an open house—frankly announced as a showing of a work in progress—is a less traumatic means of presenting the performer and presumes far less upon the good nature of the audience. Scheduling a formal dance concert and then spending class time for hurried rehearsals is like inviting the neighborhood to a birthday party and then wondering how to bake the cake just before the guests arrive.

GOALS: PHYSICAL FITNESS

Do you wish to dance as part of a personal physical fitness program? Indeed, a choreographer has to be fit in order to endure the endless task of selecting and organizing movement for a dance, but fitness itself is only a tool and not the purpose of the process. There is another kind of fitness—a unity of mind, body, emotion, and creative impulse—which serves to increase the choreographer's sense of personal well-being. This does not occur from the outside, nor is it the result of combining bits and pieces of subjects or movements. It happens on the inside as a result of continued self-actualization.

GOALS: MAKING A DANCE

Or do you simply want to make a dance? When the choreographer has an idea for a dance and cares enough about it to work tirelessly and intently on finding and forming the best possible movement, then he possesses a sound basis for starting choreography. First efforts will probably be less exciting than dances by mature artists, but we must learn to walk before we can run.

When you complete a simple and clean movement phrase, formed with sincerity, you will find that your sense of dance values is developing. This development is not merely the result of trying, but of analyzing movements, attempting alternatives, and, in the end, finding that inevitable action that seems to shine out, that you are proud of.

A PLACE TO START

TO START:
SOMETHING
TO SAY
Making a dance is very much like writing a composition: first find something to say, then say it as well as you can.

To find something to say, sharpen your perceptions of people and your world. Look and listen and then contemplate what you see and hear. Discover your interests, prejudices, and reactions. Find an idea that challenges you. No matter if the idea is based on a thrust toward imbalance, a tragic happening, a geometric design, a natural gesture, a bit of children's play, or one of a multitude of other possibilities, examine its varied aspects and implications. Think of holding a giant prism before your idea and observing every shimmering image. Find out as much as you can about it. If your idea concerns human life, go to history, literature, drama, folklore, truisms, religion, psychology, comic strips, or sociology

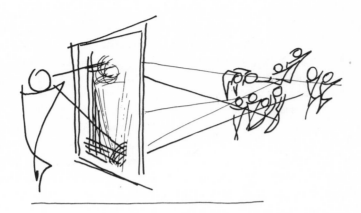

for added meaning. Search many sources, for the more you know about your idea, the wider is your scope for expressing it.

Sometimes your search will lead through a series of associated ideas that bring you, finally, to an entirely different choice of what to say. The important thing is that you are challenged and are concerned with your choice.

Select a movement to state your case. Finding a movement relevant to your idea involves a systematic exploration of the phenomena of movement, quite apart from stereotyped significance. Consider the short, concise actions of children. Here are phrases clear as crystal, uncluttered with clichés or tricks. Cut through the surface of your movement, pare it down to the core, uncover and simplify the source of reaction. Explore movement until you find a movement phrase that excites you, that seems fresh and right.

TO START: SELECTING A MOVEMENT

Impose an order on what you have to say in movement, a decided order that illuminates your point of view. Remember that you are forming a highly individual statement not restricted by common usage. You are searching for new movement symbols to express your purpose. Let your imagination wander, like that of a child who looks at a rusty nail and sees an Indian war canoe.

At first there are untold possibilities, including a myriad of movements that you have never seen or done before. You must choose among these. This is not easy, especially if you are not used to making important decisions by yourself. Other dancers may have made this choice more often and may seem more sure of themselves, but they too somehow learned to decide. Now it is up to you. The experience and the responsibility are yours.

TO START:
OUTLINING
A DANCE
STUDY
Make a dance study *in outline*. To begin your dance study, choose one movement phrase that seems important enough to be a theme. Clarify its rhythmic pattern, count the underlying beat, and make a note of it even if you just say that it is made up of three seven-counts, one nine-count, three two-counts, and a five. Be sure that you let the movement establish the count. Don't fit all of your movement to a four count unless the movement demands it.

Manipulate your movement theme in space until you have found just the right design and space relationship. Don't forget *where* and *how* the movement begins, where it goes, and where it finishes. You might make a sketch of the floor pattern so that you can study it in relation to the performance area.

Examine your dynamics, the *way* you use your energy. Jot down some clues to remind you of this. You might note, for in-

stance, that the first two seven's are smooth and sweeping, the last seven retards to static, the nine is pointed and sharp, the two's change from a lyrical run to a throb, and the five is a slow fall.

At the end of the statement of the first theme another decision must be made. Do you want to repeat it? Should there be variations on it? Or should you develop a new theme? Something must happen, but what? After you have taken the first theme where you want it to go and have manipulated other themes as well, perhaps it is time to stop! Perhaps you need a resolution and an ending.

Try to interweave your themes in such a way that recognizable bits will recur, especially if they are expressive of the purpose of the section. Remember that the audience has not experienced or seen these themes as often as you have.

After the dance is performed, ask yourself questions. Are you satisfied with the sequence, design, transitions, rhythmic structure? Were there confusions in the performance? Do you need to work on movement technique or rehearse the dance more? Would accompaniment add to it? What is an appropriate title? Would it be more exciting with more performers? How would you use them in space? If you could re-do the whole thing, what would you add, delete, or change?

BEWARE OF PITFALLS

Compromises that fill space with *any* movement
Obsession with realistic "acting out" or compromise movement
Too much or not enough contrast
Too much symmetry for no reason

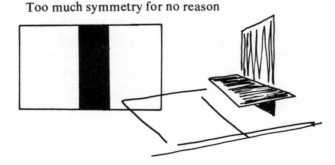

Lack of exploration and wandering from the subject

Awkward or stereotyped rhythmic or space patterns

Movement beyond the performers' ability, either in technique
or expression

Dance that goes on and on, long after its point has been made

Undue reliance on accompaniment, costuming, staging, narration, or title

Movement or design too small to be seen

Avoidance of qualified criticism

CONSIDERATIONS WORTH CONSIDERING

Was there motivation for your action? Are you satisfied that
the movements you used were relevant to the idea of the dance?
Was this a fresh exploration of the best possible action? Were you
ever surprised in its development, or did you arbitrarily use tools
of movement that you like or that "look good"?

Are you able to identify any form, or was this a wandering
statement subject to change when repeated? Did you *really* let
your imagination play, or did you merely repeat movement sequences that worked in other dances?

Was there any part that seemed weak? Is it worth changing,
or would you rather start again? Are you brave enough to forget
this effort and start all over?

Did your technique, style, or dance appearance overshadow your expression? Did you rely on personality, tricks, or gimmicks? Are you willing to let this stand as your *best* effort?

DISCRIMINATING CRITICISM

An artist must also be that threatening creature, a critic. A critic takes a piece of work and explains *why* it is good or not good. After you have made your dance, you must learn to analyze systematically what you have made. Criticism in any art form is affected by experience, sensitivity, involvement, and personal prejudice. The form and the perceived significance (and the connotations of both) assail the viewer. The initial response is usually "good" or "no good." But it is not easy to examine the reasons in either case. Try to recall what moved you. What in particular do you remember? Was there something about the dance that bothered you? Was there some apparent motive for the composition? Did it add to your awareness or change your perception?

The choreographer's intent is apt to be clearer with repeated observation and analysis of the dance, but *something* should happen between performer and audience at first showing. If the dance has any significance (not necessarily verbal), it should be shared in some part with the audience. If the dance arouses audience response, it enjoys a level of success. The more response evoked, the more successful the dance.

Unfortunately, a dance audience usually sees a dance only once; choreography, performance, and projection must succeed in this one gallant effort. There is little chance to do it better next time. For this reason, all aspects of the production must be formed, rehearsed, and closely integrated. There must be a close working relationship between choreographer, performers, designer, accompanist, and technical crew. Any one of these holds the potential for either successful performance or utter calamity.

Many in the audience are unaware of the variables that go to make up a dance concert. Fortunately, viewers usually see the performance as a total picture, but some will be disturbed by the lighting, others by the accompaniment. Some will not understand the choreography and others will dislike the costumes. The majority will react readily to the performers and their technical skill — or lack of it.

One thing is certain in any presentation, formal or informal — some of the audience will like the dances, some will not. Friends

and acquaintances will go backstage after the performance and congratulate the dancers with, "I did enjoy the program." But valid criticism that goes beyond the "I liked it" or the "I didn't like it" level is hard to come by. Discerning criticism can be of inestimable value to a choreographer if he will only listen! And his development of a critical eye when observing the choreography of others can be helpful in developing aesthetic judgment.

It is always a question if the meaning intended by the choreographer is the same as that perceived by the audience. Obviously, a dance is more successful when audience reaction bears a close resemblance to the choreographer's intent.

The beginning choreographer should devote considerable time to observing and discussing the work of other beginners and, in turn, hearing reactions to his own efforts. The following suggestions are recommended for helping the critic get started with his evaluation.

CRITICAL CUES: CONCEPTION   Did you have confidence in the choreographer's conception, in his integrity in creating this expression? Was there an apparent sincerity in the treatment of the problem? Was this expression appropriate for dance, or would it have made a better speech or poem? Did the title or program notes add or distract?

CRITICAL CUES: SELECTION   What about selection? Was the movement and development of the selected movement helpful in projecting the meaning? Was it original and fresh, or was it trite and unexciting? Was the material worth developing in dance? Was the motivation clear?

CRITICAL CUES: ORGANIZATION   Was the dance organization unified and expressive? Was the composition skillfully evolved from the stated themes? Was there a logical sequence in the development of the form? Were there too many themes? Should some of the themes have been repeated more often or developed sooner? Was there sufficient variety and contrast of action? Was the dance too long? Too short? Would you like to see something different in dynamics, rhythmic pattern, space design, relationships of dancers, floor pattern, or number of dancers?

How good was the performance? Was the necessary technique within the performers' ability? Did the technique overshadow the expression? Did the dancers have an adequate movement vocabulary and enough rehearsal? Did the personality of the dancers overpower the composition? Was there vitality and motivation? **CRITICAL CUES: PERFORMANCE**

Was projection evident? Did anything happen between the performers and the audience? Did the dancers affect the audience or just themselves? Were the performers convincing or unsure? Did they communicate the significance of the dance? **CRITICAL CUES: PROJECTION**

What were your reactions to the staging, including decor, properties, lights, costumes, and accompaniment? Did they enhance the idea of the dance or did they interfere with it? Was the accompaniment suitable for this dance? Did it overpower the movement? What would improve it? **CRITICAL CUES: STAGING**

What was your personal reaction? Did you like the dance? Did something in the form or performance disturb you? Would you like to see the dance again? Upon what bases did you approve or disapprove? Is this dance worth repeating or improving? **CRITICAL CUES: PERSONAL REACTION**

Try to analyze your feelings about all aspects of the dance. Such criticism is valuable for the choreographer, the performers, and you as a critic. When possible, offer concrete suggestions for improvement.

Probably the most important thing to consider in dance criticism is the impact of the dynamic pattern on the observer. Each one who sees the dance will have his own particular response to the interacting designs. Each member of the audience brings to the event his own personality, prejudices, remembrances, and convictions. If the dance adds *something* to his experience, it has a degree of success. If the performance results in a significant link between the choreographer's intent and the general audience response, then the choreographer has made a point!

EVALUATING YOURSELF

Last of all, an artist submits any work to his severest critic: himself. The following series of questions are springboards to self-analysis. We have said earlier that dance expresses the personality and point of view of its creator. Therefore, this *Primer* closes where all art begins and ends: with the old maxim, "Know Thyself." Your reaction to what follows will reflect your *own* attitude toward dance in general and choreography in particular. There are no "right" answers. The idea is to be completely honest about your convictions—to have the courage of them—and also to articulate your pet prejudices. The most valuable answers to these questions are the answers that are true for you.

Have you ever choreographed a complete dance?

Do you believe that there ought to be commonly accepted rules of choreography?

What, in your opinion, are the basic criteria for a "good" dance?

Do you think that there should be less analysis and talk about choreography and more time devoted to the singular act of moving?

Do you think that choreography is an intuitive process and should not be discussed?

Are choreographers born or developed?

Is choreography arranging dance steps in a pleasing sequence?

Are you satisfied with your own methods of choreographing a dance?

Do you prefer to use familiar movement that you have successfully used before?

Is this a disturbing set of questions? Do you prefer not to think about choreography, but simply to do what comes naturally?

As a choreographer, are you concerned with the audience?

Do you have a "message" to convey?

Is the message a verbal one?

Is the message nonverbal?

Is meaning in dance literal?

Are all meanings literal?

Are there meanings in dance that are not describable in words?

Are you making an expression when you choreograph?

Are you expressing yourself?

SELF-EVALUATION   Are you expressing "reality"?

Are you expressing your views of reality?

Are you concerned with "universals" in human experience?

What do you think "universals" are?

Do you enjoy interpreting a story in movement? Why?

Do you prefer interpreting music in movement? Why?

Are you concerned with a display of technical skills?

Do you depend primarily upon movement for the projection of your meaning?

Do you use program notes, titles, sets, costumes, narration, music, lights, and props as a part of your choreography?

Do you use these to clarify the meaning of the dance?

Do you use them to highlight or augment the movement?

Is all choreography creative? What does "creative" mean?

What is creative choreography characterized by?

How would you define dance as an art form?

What is your own definition of choreography?

What are the shortcomings prevalent in the choreography you have seen?

How could they be corrected?

What, for you, are the most exciting trends in contemporary choreography?

Why?

What are the shortcomings of most of the dance criticism you read?

How could they be corrected?

Describe in as much detail as possible a dance you would like
   to choreograph. (Include the idea, design, quality, num-
   ber of dancers, possible title, program notes, costume,
   accompaniment, staging, etc.)
Ideally, how would you use realistic or conventional gestures?
   Would you: Use mime or pantomime?
   Choose from natural or functional gesture?
   Organize "normal" movement to fit music?
   Adapt natural postures and acts?
   Seek dance movement out of recognizable emotions or
      moods?
   Use movement out of technical exercises?
   Use movement you like and do well?
   Use movement that is "tricky" and is sure to be applauded
      for its sparkle?
What are other alternatives?
What are other sources of movement?
How would you use exploration or improvisation?
   From a chosen attitude or mood?
   Based on words or a literal idea?
   According to personal moods or feelings?
   In response to rhythmic or melodic sounds?
   With trial-and-error movements until something pleases
      you or seems right?
   Based on space designs (such as curves and straight lines)?
   Within set time limits (such as 45 seconds)?

Guided by some aspect of dynamics (such as smooth or
                            sharp)?
                        Based on relationship of dancers (such as one against
                            three)?
                    What are other alternatives?
                    Would you develop dance form by:
                        Selecting a major movement theme and building from it?
                        Leaving it to chance?
                        Following one of the forms indicated below?
                            Theme and variation
                            Theme and development
                            Theme and contrast
                            Rondo
                            Suite
                            Fugue
                            Canon
                    Would you approach abstraction (essence) by:
                        Identifying a universal or common verbal meaning and
                            then reducing it to a movement theme?
                        Isolating a characteristic movement and then reducing it
                            to its essential movement theme?
                        Making variations on natural gesture?
                        Exploring the limits of meanings commonly associated
                            with movement and then selecting from these?
                        Keeping something of the shape, rhythm, or intent of
                            natural movement and then moving to the outer
                            limits?

What are other possibilities?

Would you start choreography by:

> Relying on personal connotations (overtones, kinaesthetic and otherwise) inherent in the act of moving?
>
> Considering the visual form of the design resulting from the dancer's action in space?
>
> Establishing a schedule of directives in space-time-force to be used?
>
> Following an intuitive urge to action?
>
> Letting one thing follow another (the "now what" approach)?

What are other possibilities?

A GLOSSARY FOR CHOREOGRAPHERS

Many of the words connected with dance, like the word "dance" itself, do not have universally accepted meanings. This glossary is certainly not a list of eternal and indisputable definitions. A number of basic aesthetic terms ("form" and "content," for instance) have been used to stand for a diversity of ideas, and more limited words (such as "self-expression" as used in these pages) may receive special definitions.

Even so, the glossary is a guide to the meanings employed in this book, and it is a starting point for the dancer as choreographer or critic. The fact that certain words may be used one way here and another way in another book should not baffle or discourage the choreographer. Rather, it should stimulate him to appreciate the richness of possible meanings and to be more effective in discovering and expressing his own ideas about dance.

ABA Form: In dance or in music, A represents one theme, B another; ABA being two contrasting themes followed by a repeat of the first.

Abstraction: The process of reducing a thing to its most basic or essential characteristics.

Accent: A display of different stress, often in contrast to what has gone before. The stress is different by its greater or lesser force.

Asymmetry: An uneven proportion in time, space, or energy, opposed to conventional balance.

Axial: Describing movement around the central axis of the body; nonlocomotor; static.

Canon: A musical term indicating a composition in which two or more parts recur, repeat, or interrelate with each other.

Circular Stage: A round or curved performance area surrounded by the audience; the stage of "theater-in-the-round."

Communication: The bridging of the gap between the performer and the audience; the successful projection of significance or intent.

Connotation: The special, often personal, meaning suggested by a word or a dance movement, aside from any common significance the word or movement possesses. This common significance is termed denotation.

Contained Movement: The result of a process of ordering or controlling the development of movement; confined action.

Contemporary Dance: The dance as a reflection of the period in which it is composed; a manifestation of the world and time in which the choreographer lives.

Content: The central concern or the intent that guides the movement formulation.

Corps de Ballet: A company of dancers prepared in the style of classical ballet.

Creativity: The process, often long and painstaking, of formulating a fresh and distinctly personal statement.

Criticism: A reasoned opinion, implying careful judgment.

Cubism: A form of artistic organization that implies that it is possible to observe and experience all aspects and levels of an object simultaneously—as if with limitless perspective.

Cumulative Rhythm: A pattern that progresses by adding units in sequence (for example, 1, 1-2, 1-2-3, 1-2-3-4).

Dance Movement: Movement that serves the purpose of any dance form is dance movement. In dance as art, movement is selected and organized on the basis of its function as a medium of expression rather than its function as work or play.

Diagonal Lines of Force: In the traditional box stage, the diagonal lines from upstage across to downstage on the other side. These lines gain force through the angles they form with each other and with the horizontal and vertical frame of the stage.

Dimension: The apparent size of a movement, relative both to previous movement and to the stage space.

Direction: A term indicating relative lines of movement; in a dance performance, the traditional forward is "out front," toward the audience, backward is away from the audience, and sideward is at a right angle to left or right.

Discrimination: A critical faculty for distinguishing relative differences and values.

Distortion: A change from the normal or average, whether by extraordinary length, complexity of movement, abruptness, or some other means.

Dynamic Image: The image that movement energy creates.

Dynamics: The energy of movement, expressed in varying intensity, accent, and quality.

Ethnic Dance: The dance of a people of common cultural, racial, and/or religious heritage. Essentially, such dance takes its time and place of performance from the culture of which it is a part; a display put on solely for tourists is ethnic in form but not in content.

Exploration: Experimental effort in the search for movement, sequence, or form.

Expressionism: The attempt of an artist to project an image on the basis of his own reaction to reality.

Focus: In general, a gathering of forces to increase the projection of intent; in particular, "focus" refers to the dancer's line of sight.

Folk Dance: The dance associated with nationalistic purpose, usually performed today as a surviving portion of a traditional celebration.

Form: The organization or plan for patterning movement; the sequence of the movement.

Fragmentation: The breaking-up or disturbing of logical relationships.

Fugue: A musical form that develops as a result of various manipulations of a given theme, often in opposition to its first statement.

Imagery: Symbols created to project a statement or emotion from imagination into visual form.

Impressionism: An artist's presentation of an oblique look at reality, as if through a cloud or mist.

Improvisation: Unplanned or extemporaneous movement.

Inertia: Tendency to remain either at rest or in motion unless some outside force intervenes.

Intensity: Presence of a greater or lesser degree of energy; relative level of energy concentration.

Jam Session: Improvisation on some established theme.

Kinaesthetic: Describing the sensations derived from nerve endings in muscle tissue; the muscle sense basic to movement awareness.

Level: An aspect of space dealing with height from the floor, ranging from a prone position to the greatest altitude of a leap; usually thought of in terms of horizontal planes.

Libretto: In dance, the libretto usually refers to the book containing the text, or verbal story, of a ballet; this story is usually combined with an identification of program sequence and the names of the performers.

Mixed Meter: A rhythmic pattern made up of irregular or regular units of different meters.

Modern Dance: Today's dance as an art form, serving to project the choreographer's intent through the medium of bodily movement, with no arbitrary restrictions on the choice of movement available to the choreographer.

Movement Theme: A formulation of movement representing a central concern or unifying intent; such a theme is the basis for development and manipulation.

Movement Transition: A sequence of movement serving to connect movement themes or phrases.

Pantomime: A dramatic performance using realistic or stylized gesture with commonly understood significance.

Pattern: The organization of materials of movement into recognizable relationships.

Perception: Conscious awareness of seeing, hearing, smelling, touching, moving, or kinaesthetic feeling.

Percussive Movement: A quality of movement characterized by sharp starts and stops; stacatto jabs of energy.

Projection: The communication of meaning to the audience. The communication is guided by the choreographer's intent and is made possible through the abilities of the dancer-performer.

Quality: The characteristics of movement determined by the way energy is used (examples are swinging, percussive, suspended, sustained, and vibratory movement).

Range: The relative scope or extent of movement; technical range of movement is determined by body size and joint flexibility.

Realism: An approach to artistic formulation that emphasizes the reproduction or duplication of "things as they are."

Rhythm: A structure of movement patterns in time.

Rondo: A musical form wherein a sequence of contrasting themes occur with an inevitable return to the first theme (for example, ABACADA).

Rubato: Literally, "robbed." In music and, by extension, in dance, the word denotes rhythmic freedom—a count taken from one measure is added to another at the performer's discretion.

Self-actualization: Attaining fulfillment of personal potential.

Self-expression: An unstructured and unformed manifestation of personal feelings.

Sense-Memory Experience: The identification of a remembered feeling, of "how it was experienced" originally.

Sequential Form: A series that develops in a prescribed succession (for example, ABA, theme and variation).

Size: Relative magnitude, established by enlarging, maintaining, or limiting the amount of space used for a movement within a given area.

Sonata: A musical form using three or four contrasting rhythms and moods that are all related in tone and style.

Space: A possibility for position and dimension; an environment necessary for any movement.

Spatial Design: The interrelationship of dancers to each other and to the space through which they are moving. This refers both to the floor area, to the space around the dancers, to the shapes they make in space, and to the space where the dancers were before they moved.

Spectacular Dance: An elaborate dance entertainment that is intended to bedazzle the audience.

Stereotyped: Lacking in individuality; produced as from a mold.

Style: A personal or characteristic manner of performing or choreographing.

Suite: A musical term describing an instrumental sequence made up of a series of forms appropriate to dance. Used in dance to indicate a sequence of related patterns or dances.

Surrealism: An artistic flight from commonplace reality, with an emphasis upon unusual, often absurd, relationships and forms.

Suspension: A quality of movement that occurs in a moment of resistance to gravity, such as the instant in which the dancer hangs in space at the top of a leap.

Sustained Movement: A quality of movement that is smooth and unaccented. There is no apparent start or stop, only a continuity of energy flow.

Swinging Movement: A quality of movement established by a fall with gravity, a gain in momentum, a loss of momentum, and the repeated cycle of fall and recovery, like that of a pendulum.

Syncopation: The displacement of the usual and expected rhythmic stress.

Technique: Movement skill.

Tempo: The pace or speed at which movement progresses; relatively slower or faster.

Theme and Variation. A form in which an initial theme is established and then followed by variations. The variations are excursions from or alternative treatments of this basic theme, without altering its essential character.

Traditional Stage: The box-shaped stage faced with a proscenium arch; the audience seated in front has a fixed perspective, and the performers project "out front" toward the audience.

Vibratory Movement: A quality of movement characterized by rapidly repeated bursts of percussive movements; like a jitter.

SELECTED READINGS

Armitage, Merle, *Martha Graham* (New York: Dance Horizons, 1966).

    Published first in 1937 and republished in 1966, this is a compilation of analyses, tributes, criticisms, and, more particularly, of developmental insights into the dance and art of Martha Graham. Written by historians, artists, critics, and colleagues, the book provides valuable references both to Miss Graham and to the new dance idiom she helped to structure. From "Affirmations 1926-1937," which represents her developing point of view, to Stark Young's essay on her early dances, each chapter adds something to the reader's understanding of dance art. There are few available references that will prove more valuable to the young choreographer.

Bruner, Jerome S., *On Knowing: Essays for the Left Hand* (Cambridge: Harvard University Press, 1962).

    Bruner's essays will be of interest to those concerned with the process of creativity and the act of discovery. Intuition, spontaneity, and feeling have long been associated with the left hand—the right with discipline, rationality, and order.

Students find this imaginative emphasis upon the attributes of the left hand to be provocative in analyzing both the process and the product of choreography.

Cane, Melville, *Making a Poem* (New York: Harvest Paperback [HB44], 1962).

   Making a Poem is essentially a personal record of the emergence of a poetic form. Cane attempts to identify the influences and unconscious factors that affected the formulation. While he is concerned with verbal form, many of his remarks, especially in the chapters called "Making a Poem," "Threshold to Creation," and "Unfinished Business," have been helpful to student choreographers.

Cary, Joyce, *Art and Reality* (New York: Anchor Paperback [A260], 1961).

   This book does not deal directly with dance, but the thirty-six short chapters on the arts in general and on the artist and his relation to the world are relevant to the developing point of view of the young dancer.

Collingwood, R. G., *The Principles of Art* (New York: Galaxy Paperback [GB11], 1963).

   The Principles of Art is not easy reading, but it has proved to be one of the most informative and helpful sources in unscrambling the rather chaotic field of art and aesthetics for my students. Art as craft, representation, magic, amusement, expression, and imagination are all examined in considerable detail. The next part of the work examines the theory of imagination, and the last section deals with the theory of art. Collingwood is valuable in helping students to define a view.

Combs, Arthur W., *et al., Perceiving, Behaving, Becoming: Yearbook of the Association for Supervision and Curriculum Development* (Washington, D.C.: National Education Association, 1962).

    Here is a clear and hopeful survey of social, psychological, and philosophical tenets dealing with the "fully functioning" and "self-actualizing" human being. Written by Arthur W. Combs, Earl C. Kelley, A. H. Maslow, and Carl R. Rogers, experts variously in psychology, education, and sociology, this yearbook provides reliable and easily understood reference to basic concepts of the creative process—to the essence of choreography.

Copland, Aaron, *Music and Imagination* (New York: Mentor Paperback [MD261], 1952).

    Copland's comments on music, on the imaginative mind, and on the role of what he has termed "musical imagination" in both traditional and contemporary musical forms are informative and appropriate for dancer and choreographer. His chapter dealing with innovations in musical form is of particular interest. The reader may frequently profit by substituting the word "dance" for "music."

Dell, Cecily, "Far Beyond the Far Out," *Dance Scope,* Vol. I,
    No. 1, Winter 1965, pp. 13-18.

> This work discusses several experimental choreographers, suggests a new relationship with the audience, and raises many questions regarding the changing face of dance. What *kinds* of meaning exist in dance? Does dance convey anything more—or less—than the visual and kinetic sensations perceived? Is the choreographer seeking to arouse a "meaning" response?

De Mille, Agnes, *The Dance* (New York: Golden Press, 1963).

> In this colorfully illustrated volume, Miss De Mille traces dance from its earliest days and presents materials of great interest to any dancer. Book III, entitled "Choreography," is particularly interesting to the young choreographer. The work includes not only ideas from great choreographers of the past and the present, but pictures of them as well.

Eliot, Alexander, *Sight and Insight* (New York: Dutton Paperback
    [D65], 1960).

> Eliot's popularly written book offers perspective and insight into many aspects of art forms. The choreographer must continually explore the realm of movement for materials of his craft, and when he stops to rest he might well read widely on art so that he may better understand himself and other artists. *Sight and Insight* provides a wide view of artistic quality and endeavor.

Gewertz, Joanna, "What Does the Choreographer Look For in a Dancer?" *Impulse 1961*, pp. 17-20.

This is a compilation of responses to the question posed in the title. Answers were gathered from active choreographers in modern dance and ballet. Rather than giving a concluding answer to the question, this article encourages the reader to evaluate both himself as a dancer and his hopes as a choreographer.

Ghiselin, Brewster, *The Creative Process* (New York: Mentor Paperback [MD132], 1958).

Here is a fascinating survey of thirty-eight brilliant men and women—all active in creative work either in the arts or in the sciences. One of them, Mary Wigman, contributed "Composition in Pure Movement," representative of her ideas of 1946. Unfortunately, it is not always possible to fix a date on the ideas of other contributors, but whatever the date, the ideas are interesting and provocative to the choreographer.

Gilbert, Pia and Aileene Lockhart, *Music for the Modern Dance* (Dubuque, Iowa: William C. Brown and Co., 1961).

Rare is the book devoted to accompaniment for dance, especially with helpful ideas for increasing rapport between accompanist and dancer. The authors have identified the basic materials necessary to understand and enhance this important relationship. Chapters 7 and 8 are particularly recommended for the young choreographer.

Gilson, Etienne, *Painting and Reality* (New York; Meridian Paper-
    back [M79], 1961).
        While this book is about painting, it has implications for
    all art forms. The close consideration of the actual works of
    painters makes clear to the reader the potential for parallels
    in other arts. The chapter called "The Significance of Modern
    Painting" is particularly relevant to dance.

Gray, Miriam, "Danger: Irascible (The Role of the Dance Ama-
    teur)," *Focus on Dance III* (Washington, D. C.: American
    Association for Health, Physical Education, and Recreation,
    National Section on Dance, National Education Association,
    1965), pp. 58-60.
        This article is of particular interest and value to the dance
    amateur, including the performer or choreographer in a school
    or semiprofessional groups. The potential as well as the dan-
    gers inherent in such activity is made clear.

Hawkins, Alma, *Creating Through Dance* (Englewood Cliffs, New
    Jersey: Prentice-Hall, 1964).
        Creating Through Dance is a scholarly and well-orga-
    nized presentation of ideas basic to the entire process of cre-
    ativity in dance. Directed mainly to the teacher and the dance
    student in academic programs, it will prove helpful to young
    dancers if they are really interested in the creative aspect of
    dance. The book considers the art of movement as a whole,
    unified by creative purpose.

Hayes, Elizabeth, *Dance Composition and Production* (New York: Ronald Press, 1955).

While this book was written mainly for the dance teacher, it is also valuable for the choreographer in developing ingenuity and a view of both choreography and production. The book suggests tools of composition and ideas for student productions. Certainly this classic for dance in education should be included on every reading list. The information offered is applicable to high schools as well as colleges.

————, *An Introduction to the Teaching of Dance* (New York: Ronald Press, 1964).

Again, here is a book directed mainly to the teacher of dance. The survey of fundamental movement and the identification of educational objectives are necessarily academic, but the author does clarify current teaching methods. The book provides references for folk and social dance as well as suggestions for accompaniment and performance.

H'Doubler, Margaret, *Dance: a Creative Art Experience* (Madison, Wisconsin: University of Wisconsin Press, 1959).

Written by one of the great educators in dance, this is an inspired and poetic presentation of the philosophy of the great lady who established the first dance major, at the University of Wisconsin in 1928. Third and fourth reading will prove more rewarding than first, for Miss H'Doubler is dealing with profound and stimulating concepts.

Horst, Louis and Carroll Russel, *Modern Dance Forms* (San Francisco: Impulse Publications, 1961).

>Louis Horst was an outstanding critic, teacher, musician, and patron of modern dance in America. Out of his vast background with Denishawn, Graham, and a host of other modern dancers, as well as his many years as teacher of dance composition to both professional dancers and teachers, he finally compiled some of his ideas on the art. With characteristic timeliness, this book really presents Mr. Horst's ideas at the moment of writing. The reader could well follow his example and use this as a starting point for personal explorations.

Humphrey, Doris, *The Art of Making Dances* (New York: Holt, Rinehart and Winston, Inc., 1959). Also available in paperback, Evergreen [E351].

>Written by one of America's great choreographers, this is a must for all young makers of dance. Principles basic to the author's approach to choreography are presented and some of the characteristics of her style are made clear.

————, "New Dance: an unfinished autobiography," *Dance Perspectives* 25, Spring 1966.

>The entire issue of the magazine is given to the story of Doris Humphrey's life up to the time when she left Denishawn. While there are no clues for the choreographer, the writing does illuminate the early years of the author's career as a great dancer and human being.

Kepes, Gyorgy, guest editor, "Statements and Documents," *Daedalus,* Winter 1960, pp. 79-120.

This is a collection of short and incisive comments by outstanding artists on art, reality, their own work, and the values associated with their work. These comments will be of great interest to the serious choreographer who is concerned with the practice of artists in many areas.

Kuh, Katherine, *Break-up: the Core of Modern Art* (New York: The Graphic Society, 1965).

This discussion of "break-up," or change in approach to the art product, will illuminate at least some questions about the relationship of form to content; about the traditional "way" in art as opposed to "a way" that develops out of the material being formed. The discussion is particularly helpful in clarifying the relationship of trends in art to the general life of the time.

Langer, Susanne K., *Feeling and Form* (New York: Charles Scribner's Sons, 1953).

This is a scholarly treatment of Langer's theory of art. Essentially it is a study in symbolism, and it is certainly no volume to pick up for light reading. Serious choreographers could profit immensely from this book, not necessarily in learning more of the process of choreography per se, but rather in understanding and organizing aesthetic concepts that have implications for dance.

————, *Problems of Art* (New York: Charles Scribner's Sons, 1957).

The ten philosophical lectures in Langer's *Problems of Art* include pivotal concepts of art theory. The first chapter contains direct reflections on dance art with particular reference to the dynamic image. The lectures as a group are an investigation of creation, expression, and experience in art, and the lectures constitute an introduction to the author's view of expressive form. A second or third reading is recommended, particularly for choreographers who wish to pursue the ramifications of an influential theory.

————, editor, *Reflections on Art* (New York: Galaxy Paperback [GB60], 1961).

Susanne Langer has edited a valuable collection of significant essays on art by outstanding artists, critics, and philosophers. Here is another opportunity for dancers and choreographers to find greater perspective on and insight into artistic expression.

Lippincott, Gertrude, "The Magic of Performance," *Focus on Dance III* (Washington, D. C.: American Association for Health, Physical Education, and Recreation, National Section on Dance, National Education Association, 1965), p. 17.

What happens between the audience and the performer? Mrs. Lippincott, dancer, choreographer, teacher, and writer, has some suggestions that are most relevant for the young choreographer and performer.

Lockhart, Aileene and Esther Pease, *Modern Dance: Building and Teaching Lessons* (Dubuque, Iowa: William C. Brown and Co., 1966).

This new edition of a well-known aid to both teachers and dance students will be of interest to all young choreographers. It surveys the approaches to the technique of moving and the process of organizing movement into dances.

Martin, John, *Introduction to the Dance* (New York: Dance Horizons, 1963).

This is a reprint of a classic work first published in 1939. "The Dance in Theory" and "The Dance in Action" represent the framework of the point of view held by this most famous of all dance critics. Almost thirty years later, much of the writing is still applicable and helpful in understanding the changes and trends of today's dance.

Metheny, Eleanor, *Connotations of Movement in Sport and Dance* (Dubuque, Iowa: William C. Brown and Co., 1965).

While the entire book can add to the depth of understanding about movement experiences, the following sections are particularly relevant for the choreographer: "Symbolic Forms of Movement: Dance," "Athletics in the Studio," "The Search for Meaning in Movement," and "An Inquiry into the Nature of Movement as Significant Form." Many of the questions that besiege the young choreographer are both asked and answered, notably, "What does the movement mean?"

————, *Movement and Meaning* (New York: McGraw-Hill Book Co., in press, with probable publication in 1968).

Here is a masterful clarification of dance, sport, and exercise. The common elements as well as the differentiating factors are identified. More importantly, a working philosophy of movement and meaning is made evident. This marks a new point of reference for all choreographers and for others concerned with the potential of movement.

Moffett, James, "The Second Person," *Impulse 1962*, pp. 32-36.

Concerned with a theory of communication, Moffett turns to the performing arts and suggests a significant series of changes in the relation of performer to his audience. He develops an interesting theory that applies to the choreographer of today.

Moulton, Robert, "The Meaning of Gesture," *Focus on Dance III* (Washington, D.C.: American Association for Health, Physical Education, and Recreation, National Section on Dance, National Education Association, 1965), pp. 31-33.

Here is a personal affirmation of the need for communication in the movement of dance and an attempt to clarify just what is meant by communication. The article is not suggested as a reading for acquiring a particular knowledge about movement, but rather as a source of motivation by which the young choreographer may discover what is meaningful in movement.

Myers, Martha and Gerald, "On Creativity," *Focus on Dance III* (Washington, D. C.: American Association for Health, Physical Education, and Recreation, National Section on Dance, National Education Association, 1965), pp. 12-14.

   This is a short, yet illuminating article on the very nature of creativity, with some implications for the considerable confusion that arises from that term.

Pease, Esther, "Epilogue – A Conversation with Louis Horst," *Impulse 1965*, pp. 4-5.

   In this report of a conversation between Louis Horst and the author, Mr. Horst evaluates the young dancer of today and sheds considerable light on the need for hard work and analysis.

Philipson, Morris, editor, *Aesthetics Today* (New York: Meridian Paperback [M112], 1961).

   This is a highly selective compilation of readings representative of issues currently stimulating critics, philosophers, and artists. The book is another of the sources for broadening the artistic eye of the young choreographer.

Pischl, A. J., editor, "Composer/Choreographer," *Dance Perspectives* 16, 1963.

   This entire issue of *Dance Perspectives* is devoted to the relationship of music to choreography. Eleven contemporary musicians present their views on the interaction of music and dance, and especially their role as composers for dance. Not only will the reader learn of practices in forming musical compositions, but he will also discover something of the philosophies of those who compose the music.

Read, Herbert, *Icon and Idea* (Cambridge: Harvard University Press, 1955).

The basis for Read's theory of symbolization is presented in this valuable book. Whatever art form is concerned, the bases for identifying significance in the form are explored. Certainly no one has presented a clearer analysis of symbolization in art.

————, *The Philosophy of Modern Art* (New York: Meridian Paperback [M7] , 1957).

Here is a collection of essays prepared by one of the most prolific and renowned experts on the arts of man. It is of interest to the choreographer today because it clarifies and exposes many aspects of modern art and adds insight to the contributions of some of the leading contemporary artists.

————, *The Forms of Things Unknown* (New York: Meridian Paperback [M168], 1963).

Problems that involve over-all aesthetic principles, especially as they interact in a technological world, are discussed and evaluated in the light of the deep experience and insight of the author.

————, *The Grass Roots of Art* (New York: Meridian Paperback [M108], 1961).

This book contains a series of lectures on the social aspects of art in the modern world. Of special interest to the young artist is the chapter entitled "The Roots of the Artist." "The Aesthetic Method of Education" presents Read's concept of the developmental pattern of aesthetic sensitivity. The reader will learn little of the direct process of choreography, but may increase his ability to organize concepts about art and find meaning in them.

Rugg, Harold, *Imagination* (New York: Harper and Row, 1963).

This is both an inquiry into the sources and conditions that stimulate creative endeavor and a synthesis and interpretation of theory and research into the act of creation. It is recommended that Chapter 15, dealing with creative imagination, be read first.

Santayana, George, *The Sense of Beauty* (New York: Collier Paperback [BS34YV], 1961).

A philosophical treatise outlining aesthetic theory, this represents another aspect of the analysis of art. The book is divided into four major parts: "The Nature of Beauty," "The Materials of Beauty," "Form," and "Expression." Again, this work does not deal with the specific areas of choreography, but it does represent a valid point of view that will add to the knowledge of young artists.

Shahn, Ben, *The Shape of Content* (New York: Vintage Paperback [V108], 1957).

    Shahn is a teacher, critic, and writer, as well as an active and prolific painter of our time. He is author of the phrase, "Form is the visible shape of content." This book extends from this quotation and provides discussions most appropriate for the choreographer.

Sheets, Maxine, *The Phenomenology of Dance* (Madison, Wisconsin: University of Wisconsin Press, 1966).

    Here is a scholarly treatment of dance as art and education from a phenomenological point of view—that is, the book presents a descriptive analysis of dance's existence. Certainly not easy reading, the book does offer the challenge of a penetrating dissection of the dance experience. The serious choreographer will find many interesting insights in the treatment of dance as a human activity subject to phenomenological description.

Smith, Nancy W., "The Critical Function," *Focus on Dance III* (Washington, D.C.: American Association for Health, Physical Education, and Recreation, National Section on Dance, National Education Association, 1965), pp. 61-64.

    Miss Smith has briefly traced the picture of dance criticism in this country and has identified some of the characteristics of the critics who have helped to clarify the developing art form.

Sorell, Walter, "The Meaning of Man as an Artist," *Focus on Dance II* (Washington, D. C.: American Association for Health, Physical Education, and Recreation, National Section on Dance, National Education Association, 1962), pp. 31-39.

One of the great dance critics writes of the dancer as an artist and of his problems in the world of art. The "Conversations" following the article are of special interest.

————, *The Dance Has Many Faces* (New York: Columbia University Press, 1966).

This collection of essays on dance by dancers, critics, and other artists not only helps to clarify the role of dance in our world, but also to illuminate the point of view of the artists concerned.

Stodelle, Ernestine, "Revolution or Evolution," *Impulse 1966*, pp. 6-8.

Miss Stodelle questions the basis for verbal blasts at either "traditional" or "anti-dance" approaches to composition. She points out the confusions in the alleged conflict between approaches. "Where, then, is the revolution?" she asks.

Wooten, Bettie Jane, editor, "Report: Theories of Movement," *Focus on Dance II* (Washington, D. C.: American Association for Health, Physical Education, and Recreation, National Section on Dance, National Education Association, 1962), pp. 5-29.

120

SELECTED READINGS

Six basic theories of movement are discussed, each relevant to the concerns of the young choreographer, though not to the process of choreography directly.

Yates, Peter, "Merce Cunningham Restores the Dance to Dance," *Impulse 1965*, pp. 13-17.

This is a report of both early and later work of Cunningham, often described as one of the most modern of the "moderns." Casual observations, discussions of the intent of some works, and plans for the future are included.

ABOUT THE AUTHOR

Lois Ellfeldt is Chairman of the Dance Major and Professor of Physical Education and Education at the University of Southern California. She has been Treasurer, Secretary, and Chairman of the Dance Division of the American Association for Health, Physical Education, and Recreation, and she has served as lecturer, performer, consultant, teacher, and member of professional committees on dance.

After receiving her M.S. from Wellesley College, she danced with the Doris Humphrey – Charles Weidman Company, organized her own performing group in Washington, D.C., attended the Bennington College Summer School of Dance, and then taught at the University of California, Berkeley. She received her Ph.D. degree from the University of Southern California in 1946. During her tenure there she has been responsible for thirty major dance productions.